MORE EVERYDAY LEGAL FORMS

2nd Edition

by
Margaret C. Jasper

Oceana's Legal Almanac Series
Law for the Layperson

2001
Oceana Publications, Inc.
Dobbs Ferry, New York

Library of Congress Control Number 2001135859

ISBN: 0-379-11361-9

Oceana's Legal Almanac Series: Law for the Layperson
ISSN 1075-7376

To My Husband Chris

Your love and support
are my motivation and inspiration

-and-

In memory of my son, Jimmy

Table of Contents

CHAPTER 8
PERSONAL RELATIONSHIPS

CHAPTER 9
REAL ESTATE AND LANDLORD-TENANT MATTERS

ABOUT THE AUTHOR

MARGARET C. JASPER is an attorney engaged in the general practice of law in South Salem, New York, concentrating in the areas of personal injury and entertainment law. Ms. Jasper holds a Juris Doctor degree from Pace University School of Law, White Plains, New York, is a member of the New York and Connecticut bars, and is certified to practice before the United States District Courts for the Southern and Eastern Districts of New York, the United States Court of Appeals for the Second Circuit, and the United States Supreme Court.

Ms. Jasper has been appointed to the panel of arbitrators of the American Arbitration Association and the law guardian panel for the Family Court of the State of New York, is a member of the Association of Trial Lawyers of America, and is a New York State licensed real estate broker and member of the Westchester County Board of Realtors, operating as Jasper Real Estate, in South Salem, New York. Margaret Jasper maintains a website at http://members.aol.com/JasperLaw.

Ms. Jasper is the author and general editor of the following legal almanacs: Juvenile Justice and Children's Law; Marriage and Divorce; Estate Planning; The Law of Contracts; The Law of Dispute Resolution; Law for the Small Business Owner; The Law of Personal Injury; Real Estate Law for the Homeowner and Broker; Everyday Legal Forms; Dictionary of Selected Legal Terms; The Law of Medical Malpractice; The Law of Product Liability; The Law of No-Fault Insurance; The Law of Immigration; The Law of Libel and Slander; The Law of Buying and Selling; Elder Law; The Right to Die; AIDS Law; The Law of Obscenity and Pornography; The Law of Child Custody; The Law of Debt Collection; Consumer Rights Law; Bankruptcy Law for the Individual Debtor; Victim's Rights Law; Animal Rights Law; Workers' Compensation Law; Employee Rights in the Workplace; Probate Law; Environmental Law; Labor Law; The Americans with Disabilities Act; The Law of Capital Punishment; Education Law; The Law of Violence Against Women; Landlord-Tenant

Law; Insurance Law; Religion and the Law; Commercial Law; Motor Vehicle Law; Social Security Law; The Law of Drunk Driving; The Law of Speech and the First Amendment; Employment Discrimination Under Title VII; Hospital Liability Law; Home Mortgage Law Primer; Copyright Law; Patent Law; Trademark Law; Special Education Law; The Law of Attachment and Garnishment; Banks and their Customers; and Credit Cards and the Law.

CHAPTER 1
ARBITRATION AND MEDIATION

FORM 1-1

AGREEMENT TO SUBMIT A DISPUTE TO ARBITRATION

We, the undersigned parties, hereby agree to submit to arbitration administered by the American Arbitration Association under its Commercial Arbitration Rules the following controversy: *[describe nature of dispute]*.

We further agree that the above controversy be submitted to three arbitrators.

We further agree that we will faithfully observe this agreement and the rules, and that we will abide by and perform any award rendered by the arbitrators and that a judgment of the court having jurisdiction may be entered on the award.

DATED: BY: _____

DATED: BY: _____

FORM 1-2

CONTRACT ARBITRATION CLAUSE

Any controversy or claim arising out of or relating to this contract, or the breach thereof, shall be settled by arbitration administered by the American Arbitration Association in accordance with its Commercial Arbitration Rules, and judgment on the award rendered by the arbitrator(s) may be entered in any court having jurisdiction thereof.

FORM 1-3

AGREEMENT TO SUBMIT A DISPUTE TO MEDIATION

The parties hereby submit the following dispute to mediation administered by the American Arbitration Association under its commercial Mediation rules. (Describe nature of dispute and may also detail the qualifications of the mediator(s), method of payment, locale of meetings and any other item of concern to the parties).

DATED: BY: _____

DATED: BY: _____

FORM 1-4

CONTRACT MEDIATION CLAUSE

If a dispute arises out of or relates to this contract, or the breach thereof, and if said dispute cannot be settled through negotiation, the parties agree first to try in good faith to settle the dispute by mediation administered by the American Arbitration Association under its Commercial Mediation Rules, before resorting to arbitration, litigation, or some other dispute resolution procedure.

FORM 1-5

DEMAND FOR ARBITRATION

Date:

To: (Name of the Party on Whom the Demand is Made)

Address:

Telephone:

Fax:

Name of Representative: (if known)

Name of Firm: (if Applicable)

Representative's Address:

Telephone:

Fax:

The named claimant, a party to an arbitration agreement contained in a written contract, dated _____ and providing for arbitration under the Voluntary Arbitration Rules of the American Arbitration Association, hereby demands arbitration thereunder. (Attach the arbitration clause or quote it hereunder.)

NATURE OF DISPUTE:

CLAIM OR RELIEF SOUGHT: (amount, if any):

HEARING LOCALE REQUESTED: (City and State)

You are hereby notified that copies of our arbitration agreement and this demand are being filed with the American Arbitration Association at its _____ office, with a request that it commence administration of the arbitration. Under the rules, you may file an answering statement within ten days after notice from the administrator.

Signed_____

Title: (may be signed by representative)

Name of Claimant:

Address: (to Be Used in Connection with this Case)

Telephone:

Fax:

Name of Representative

Representative's Address

Telephone:

Fax:

To institute proceedings, please send three copies of this demand and the arbitration agreement, with the filing fee as provided in the rules, to the AAA. Send the original demand to the respondent.

FORM 1-6

FORM FOR SUBMITTING A DISPUTE FOR RESOLUTION

The named parties hereby submit the following dispute for resolution under the applicable Rules of the American Arbitration Association.

Procedure Selected:

    Binding Arbitration ____

    Mediation Settlement ____

    Other (Please describe)_____

THE NATURE OF THE DISPUTE

THE CLAIM OR RELIEF SOUGHT (the Amount, if Any):

TYPE OF BUSINESS:

    Claimant _____

    Respondent _____

    PLACE OF HEARING:

We agree that, if binding arbitration is selected, we will abide by and perform any award rendered hereunder and that a judgement may be entered on the award.

To Be Completed by the Parties

Signed_____

Name of Party:

Address:

Telephone:

Fax:

Signed_____

Name of Party:

Address:

Telephone:

Fax:

Signed_____

Name of Representative of: (state which party)

Representative's Address

Telephone:

Fax:

Signed_____

Name of Representative of: (state which party)

Representative's Address

Telephone:

Fax:

Please file three copies with the AAA

If you have a question as to which rules apply, please contact the AAA.

Signatures of all parties are required for arbitration.

FORM 1-7

REQUEST FOR MEDIATION

Date:

To: (Name of the Party on Whom the Demand is Made)

Address:

Telephone:

Fax:

The undersigned party to an agreement contained in a written contract dated _____, providing for mediation under the Mediation Rules of the American Arbitration Association, hereby requests mediation thereunder. (Attach the mediation clause or quote it hereunder.)

NATURE OF DISPUTE:

THE CLAIM OR RELIEF SOUGHT: (the amount, if any)

TYPE OF BUSINESS:

　　Filing Party _____

　　Responding Party _____

MEDIATION LOCALE REQUESTED:

You are hereby notified that copies of our mediation agreement and of this request are being filed with the American Arbitration Association office, with the request that it commence the administration of the mediation.

Signed_____

Title: (may be signed by representative)

Name of Filing Party:

Address: (to Be Used in Connection with this Case)

Telephone:

Fax:

Name of Representative

Representative's Address

Telephone:

Fax:

To institute proceedings, please send three copies of this request with the administrative fee, as provided for in the rules, to the AAA. Send the original request to the responding party.

If you have a question as to which rules apply, please contact the AAA.

CHAPTER 2
CONTRACTS

FORM 2-1

BILL OF SALE

I, *[Name of Seller]* ("Seller"), of *[Address]* do hereby sell, assign and transfer to *[Name of Buyer]* ("Buyer"), of *[Address]*, the following property:

[Specify property to be sold in detail, including, if applicable, model no(s), serial no(s), and other identifying information]

The above property is sold on an "as is" basis. The Seller makes no warranties, express or implied (except as specifically stated herein). *[If a warranty is desired, specify, e.g.: "that the item remain in good working order for a minimum of 30 days from the date of sale"]*.

This transfer is effective as of *[Date]*.

The property is now located at *[Specify location of property to be transferred]*, in the possession of the Seller.

DATED: BY: _____
                                   [SIGNATURE LINE—SELLER]

DATED: BY: _____
                                   [SIGNATURE LINE—BUYER]

FORM 2-2

BILL OF SALE—MOTOR VEHICLE

SELLER'S NAME AND ADDRESS:

In consideration of the payment of the sum of *[Insert Dollar Amount ($xxx)]*, I do hereby sell to:

BUYER'S NAME AND ADDRESS:

The following motor vehicle:

YEAR/MAKE/MODEL:

VIN#:

MILEAGE:

OTHER INFORMATION:

DATED: BY: _____
                                [SELLER'S SIGNATURE LINE]

FORM 2-3

BREACH OF CONTRACT NOTIFICATION

DATE:

TO: *[Name and Address of Contractor]*

FROM: *[Name and Address of Homeowner]*

RE: BREACH OF AGREEMENT DATED *[DATE OF CONTRACT]*

SIR/MADAM:

On *[Insert Date of Contract]*, we entered into a written agreement which provided that *[Insert Name of Contractor]* would build a deck for my home according to the specifications provided by me. A copy of the fully-executed agreement is attached.

According to our agreement, you were to begin work on the deck no later than 7 calendar days following the execution of the agreement. Since the agreement was executed on *[Insert Date of Contract]*, work was to begin on the deck no later than *[Insert Date of Contract + 7 days)*.

Additionally, you were to complete work on the deck within 45 calendar days following the execution of the agreement, thus, the deck should have been completed on or before *[Insert Date of Contract + 45 days)*.

Please take notice that you are now in breach of your obligations contained in that agreement in that as of this date *[Insert Present Date]*, you have not begun work on the deck, and that this failure to comply with the terms of our agreement is due solely to the negligence of *[Insert Name of Contractor]*.

Please be further advised that I intend to hold you responsible for all actual and consequential damages arising from your breach, including but not limited to liquidated damages in the amount set forth in our agreement.

BY: _____
                [SIGNATURE LINE—HOMEOWNER]

FORM 2-4

CONTRACT FOR SERVICES—HOMEOWNER/CONTRACTOR

THIS AGREEMENT is hereby entered into this ___ day of _____, 20__, between *[Name and Address]* ("Homeowner"), and *[Name and Address]* ("Contractor").

The above parties, for the consideration set forth below, hereby agree as follows:

1. Contractor agrees to build a deck for Homeowner in the exact dimensions and specifications set forth on the attached Exhibit A, which is made a part of this agreement.

2. Contractor agrees to provide and pay for all labor and materials necessary to complete the deck.

3. Homeowner agrees to pay Contractor the sum of *[Dollar Amount ($xxx)]* Dollars as and for compensation for labor and materials, payable as follows:

(a) *[Dollar Amount ($xxx)]* Dollars upon signing this agreement; and

(b) *[Dollar Amount ($xxx)]* Dollars when the deck is 50% completed; and

(c) *[Dollar Amount ($xxx)]* Dollars upon completion of the deck.

4. Contractor agrees that they will begin work on the deck within seven (7) calendar days from the date the contract is signed; and that the deck shall be completed within forty-five (45) calendar days from the date of contract.

5. Homeowner and Contractor agree that time is of the essence in completion of this deck, therefore, if the deck is not completed by the date set forth herein due to the neglect of the Contractor, Contractor agrees to pay Homeowner the sum of *[Dollar amount ($xxx)]* Dollars per day as liquidated damages until such time as the work is completed.

6. Notwithstanding Paragraph 5 of this agreement, in the event Contractor is delayed from completing the deck due to an act of God, fire, flood or other unavoidable event, or by fault of Homeowner, the date of completion shall be extended accordingly.

7. This contract contains the entire understanding between Homeowner and Contractor and any changes to this contract must be in writing and signed by both parties.

8. This contract is not assignable without the written consent of both parties.

9. This contract is governed by the laws of the State of *[Name of State]*.

10. The invalidity, in whole or in part, of any term of this agreement does not affect the validity of the remainder of the agreement.

BY: _____

[SIGNATURE LINE—HOMEOWNER]

BY: _____

[SIGNATURE LINE—CONTRACTOR]

FORM 2-5

GENERAL ASSIGNMENT OF CONTRACT

LET IT BE KNOWN that, for value received, *[Name of Assignor]* ("Assignor"), hereby assigns, transfers and sets over to *[Name of Assignee]* ("Assignee"), all right, title and interest held by Assignor in and to a contract *[set forth details of contract being assigned, e.g.: between Assignor and Mary Jones ("Seller") dated January 1, 20__ providing for the sale of a 1997 Ford Taurus automobile by Seller to Assignor for the sum of Ten Thousand ($10,000), as more fully set forth in said contract, a copy of which is attached hereto and made a part of this assignment].*

Assignor hereby warrants and represents that said contract is fully assignable and in full force.

Assignee hereby assumes and agrees to perform all remaining obligations of Assignor under the contract, if any, and agrees to indemnify and hold Assignor harmless from any claim against Assignor arising from non-performance of the contract by Assignee.

Assignor further warrants that he has the full right and authority to transfer said contract, and that the rights herein transferred are free of lien and encumbrance of any kind whatsoever.

This assignment shall be binding upon and inure to the benefit of the parties, their successors and assigns.

DATE: BY: _____
                           [SIGNATURE LINE—ASSIGNOR]

DATE: BY: _____
                           [SIGNATURE LINE—ASSIGNEE]

FORM 2-6

EQUIPMENT LEASE

This Equipment Lease (the "Lease") is made effective as of *[Date]* between *[Name and Address]* (the "Lessor"), and *[Name and Address]* (the "Lessee"), and states the agreement of the parties as follows:

1. The Lessor shall lease the equipment listed on the attached Exhibit A (the "Equipment Schedule").

2. The Lessee shall make *[Specify manner in which payments shall be made, e.g.: 12 payments of $200 each]*.

3. Payments shall be due on the *[e.g., first]* day of each *[e.g., month]* with the first payment due on *[Date]*.

4. The lease payments shall be due whether or not the Lessee has received notice of a payment due.

5. The Lessee shall be charged *[Dollar Amount ($xxx)]* for each check that is returned to the Lessor for lack of sufficient funds.

6. In addition to the lease payment charge, the Lessee shall pay a security deposit of *[Dollar Amount (xxx)]* at the time that this Lease is signed. This deposit will be returned to the Lessee at the termination of this Lease, subject to the option of the Lessor to apply it against Lease charges and damages. Any amounts refundable to the Lessee shall be paid within *[No. of days]* after this Lease is terminated. The security deposit shall not bear interest.

7. The Lessee assumes all risks of loss or damage to the equipment from any cause, and agrees to return it to the Lessor in the condition received from the Lessor, with the exception of normal wear and tear.

8. This Lease shall begin on the above effective date and shall terminate on *[Date]*.

9. The equipment shall be located at *[Address]* during the lease term, and shall not be removed from that location without the Lessor's prior written consent.

10. The equipment shall be used and operated in a careful and proper manner. Its use must comply with all laws, ordinances, and regulations

relating to the possession, use, or maintenance of the equipment, including registration and/or licensing requirements, if any.

11. The Lessee shall maintain the equipment in good repair and operating condition, allowing for reasonable wear and tear. The Lessee shall pay all costs required to maintain the equipment in good operating condition. Such costs shall include labor, material, parts, and similar items.

12. The Lessor shall have the right to inspect the equipment during Lessee's normal business hours.

13. At the end of the Lease term, the Lessee shall be obligated to return the equipment to the Lessor at the Lessee's expense.

14. If the Lessee is not in default upon the expiration of this lease, the Lessee shall have first option to lease the equipment on such terms as the parties may agree at that time.

15. If the Lessee is not in default under this Lease, the Lessee shall have the option to purchase items of equipment at the end of the lease term for the price specified for such items of equipment in the attached Equipment Schedule. The Lessee shall exercise this option by providing written notice to the Lessor of such intent at least *[No. of Days]* prior to the end of the lease term.

16. The Lessee shall inspect each item of equipment delivered pursuant to this lease. The Lessee shall immediately notify the Lessor of any discrepancies between such item of equipment and the description of the equipment in the Equipment Schedule. If the Lessee fails to provide such notice before accepting delivery of the equipment, the Lessee will be conclusively presumed to have accepted the equipment as specified in the Equipment Schedule.

17. The equipment will be deemed to be personal property, regardless of the manner in which it may be attached to any other property.

18. The Lessor shall be deemed to have retained title to the equipment at all times, unless the Lessor transfers the title by sale.

19. The Lessee shall immediately advise the Lessor regarding any notice of any claim, levy, lien, or legal process issued against the equipment.

20. The Lessor warrants that the above property is in good working condition, but makes no further warranties, express or implied.

21. If the equipment is damaged or lost, the Lessor shall have the option of requiring the Lessee to repair the equipment to a state of good working order, or replace the equipment with like equipment in good re-

pair, which equipment shall become the property of the Lessor and subject to this Lease.

22. Liability for injury, disability, and death of workers and other persons caused by operating, handling, or transporting the equipment during the term of this Lease is the obligation of the Lessee, and the Lessee shall indemnify and hold the Lessor harmless from and against all such liability.

23. The Lessee shall insure the equipment in an amount of at least *[Dollar Amount ($xxx) Dollars]*.

24. During the term of this Lease, the Lessee shall pay all taxes, assessments, and license and registration fees on the equipment.

25. The occurrence of any of the following shall constitute a default under this Lease:

(a) The failure to make a required payment under this Lease when due.

(b) The violation of any other provision or requirement that is not corrected within *[No. of Days]* after written notice of the violation is given.

(c) The insolvency or bankruptcy of the Lessee.

(d) The subjection of any of Lessee's property to any levy, seizure, assignment, application or sale for or by any creditor or government agency.

26. If the Lessee is in default under this Lease, without notice to or demand on the Lessee, the Lessor may take possession of the equipment as provided by law, deduct the costs of recovery (including attorney fees and legal costs), repair, and related costs, and hold the Lessee responsible for any deficiency. The Lessor shall be obligated to re-lease the equipment, or otherwise mitigate the damages from the default, only as required by law.

27. All notices required or permitted under this Lease shall be deemed delivered when delivered in person or by mail, postage prepaid, addressed to the appropriate party at the address shown for that party at the beginning of this Lease.

28. The Lessee shall not assign or sublet any interest in this Lease or the equipment or permit the equipment to be used by anyone other than the Lessee or Lessee's employees, without Lessor's prior written consent.

29. This Lease constitutes the entire agreement between the parties. No modification or amendment of this Lease shall be effective unless in writing and signed by both parties. This Lease replaces any and all prior agreements between the parties.

30. This Lease shall be construed in accordance with the laws of the State of *[Name of State]*.

31. If any portion of this Lease shall be held to be invalid or unenforceable for any reason, the remaining provisions shall continue to be valid and enforceable. If a court finds that any provision of this Lease is invalid or unenforceable, but that by limiting such provision, it would become valid and enforceable, then such provision shall be deemed to be written, construed, and enforced as so limited.

32. The failure of either party to enforce any provision of this Lease shall not be construed as a waiver or limitation of that party's right to subsequently enforce and compel strict compliance with every provision of this Lease.

33. Lessee certifies that the application, statements, trade references, and financial reports submitted to Lessor are true and correct and any material misrepresentation will constitute a default under this Lease.

DATED: BY: _____
                              [SIGNATURE LINE—LESSOR]

DATED: BY: _____
                              [SIGNATURE LINE—LESSEE]

ATTACHMENT:

EXHIBIT A
Equipment Schedule

Description of Equipment:

FORM 2-7

CONSTRUCTION LIEN CLAIM FORM

TO THE CLERK, COUNTY OF _____:

In accordance with the terms and provisions of the [applicable statute], notice is hereby given that:

1. (Name of claimant) of (address of claimant) has on (date) claimed a construction lien against the below stated real property of (owner against whose property the lien is claimed), in the amount of ($), for the value of the work, services, material or equipment provided in accordance with a contract with (name of contracting party with whom claimant has a contract) for the following work, services, materials or equipment:

[Details of work, services, material or equipment]

2. The amount due for work, services, materials or equipment delivery provided by claimant in connection with the improvement of the real property, and upon which this lien claim is based, is as follows:

Total contract amount: $

Amendments to contract: $

Total contract amount and amendments to contract: $

Less:

Agreed upon credits: $

Contract amount paid to date: $

Amendments to contract amount paid to date: $

TOTAL REDUCTIONS FROM CONTRACT AMOUNT AND AMENDMENTS TO CONTRACT: $

TOTAL LIEN CLAIM AMOUNT: $

Notice of Unpaid Balance and Right to File Lien (if any) was previously filed with the County Clerk of County on [Date] as #____ in Book#____ Page#____.

3. This construction lien is claimed against the interest of (name) as (check one):

Owner

Lessee

Other (describe):

in that certain tract or parcel of land and premises described as Block#___, Lot#___, on the tax map of the _____ County, State of _____, for the improvement of which property the aforementioned work, services, materials or equipment was provided.

4. The work, services, materials or equipment was provided pursuant to the terms of a written contract (or, in the case of a supplier, a delivery or order slip signed by the owner, contractor, or subcontractor having a direct contractual relation with a contractor, or an authorized agent of any of them), dated, between (claimant) and (name of other contracting party) of (address).

5. The date of the provision of the last work, services, material or equipment for which payment is claimed is (date).

NOTICE TO OWNER OF REAL PROPERTY

Your real estate may be subject to sale to satisfy the amount asserted by this claim. However, your real estate cannot be sold until the facts and issues which form the basis of this claim are decided in a legal proceeding before a court of law. The lien claimant is required by law to commence suit to enforce this claim.

The claimant filing this lien claim shall forfeit all rights to enforce the lien and shall be required to discharge the lien of record, if the claimant fails to bring an action in the Superior Court, in the county in which the real property is situated, to establish the lien claim:

1. Within one year of the date of the last provision of work, services, material or equipment, payment for which the lien claim was filed; or

2. Within 30 days following receipt of written notice, by personal service or certified mail, return receipt requested, from the owner requiring the claimant to commence an action to establish the lien claim.

You will be given proper notice of the proceeding and an opportunity to challenge this claim and set forth your position. If, after you (and/or your contractor or subcontractor) have had the opportunity to challenge this lien claim, the court of law enters a judgment against you and in favor of the claimant filing this lien claim, and thereafter you fail to pay that judgment, your real estate may then be sold to satisfy the judgment.

You may choose to avoid subjecting your real estate to sale by doing either of the following:

1. You (or your contractor or subcontractor) can pay the claimant and obtain a discharge of lien claim from the claimant; or

2. You (or your contractor or subcontractor) can cause the lien claim to be discharged by filing a surety bond or making a deposit of funds as provided for in [cite applicable law]).

If you (or your contractor or subcontractor) choose to pay the claimant under 1. above, you will lose your right to challenge this lien claim in a legal proceeding before a court of law.

If you (or your contractor or subcontractor) choose to discharge the lien claim by filing a surety bond or making a deposit of funds as provided in [cite applicable law], you will retain your right to challenge this lien claim in a legal proceeding before a court of law.

NOTICE TO SUBCONTRACTOR OR CONTRACTOR:

This lien has been filed with the county clerk and served upon the owner of the real estate. This lien places the owner on notice that the real estate may be sold to satisfy this claim unless the owner pays the claimed sum to this claimant.

[Date and Signature Lines]

CLAIMANT'S REPRESENTATION AND VERIFICATION

Claimant represents and verifies that:

1. The amount claimed herein is due and owing at the date of filing, pursuant to claimant's contract described in the construction lien claim.

2. The work, services, material or equipment for which this lien claim is filed was provided exclusively in connection with the improvement of the real property which is the subject of this claim.

3. This claim has been filed within 90 days from the last date upon which the work, services, materials or equipment for which payment is claimed was provided.

4. The foregoing statements made by me are true, to the best of my knowledge. I am aware that if any of the foregoing statements made by me are false, this construction lien claim will be void and that I will be liable for damages to the owner or any other person injured as a consequence of the filing of this lien claim.

[Name and Signature Line for Claimant]

[Date]

CHAPTER 3
CORPORATIONS AND BUSINESS ASSOCIATIONS

FORM 3-1

BUSINESS CERTIFICATE

I hereby certify that I am conducting or transacting business under the name or designation of [Name of Company], at [address of Company].

My full name is [Name of Owner], and I reside at [Owner's Address].

IN WITNESS WHEREOF, I have made and signed this certificate on [date].

Signature Line for Owner

STATE OF

COUNTY OF

On [date], before me personally came [owner's name], to me known to be the person described in and who executed the foregoing instrument and duly acknowledged to me that (s)he executed the same.

Signature Line for Notary

FORM 3-2

CORPORATE MINUTES OF *[NAME OF CORPORATION]*

A regular meeting of the Board of Directors of the above corporation was held on *[Date]* at the corporation's place of business.

The purpose of the meeting *[Specify purpose for which meeting was called]*.

1. QUORUM. A quorum was declared present based on the presence of the following directors:

Director: *[Name]*

Director: *[Name]*

[Add additional names as applicable].

and the following shareholders as owners of the following shares of stock:

Shareholder: *[Name]*

Number of Shares: *[Specify Number, e.g. 50]*

Appeared: *[Specify "in person" or "by proxy"]*

Shareholder: *[Name]*

Number of Shares: *[Specify Number, e.g. 50]*

Appeared: *[Specify "in person" or "by proxy"]*

[Add additional names as applicable].

The following corporate actions were taken by appropriate motions duly made, seconded, and adopted by the *[xx%]* vote of the Directors entitled to vote.

2. ELECTION OF CHAIRPERSON AND SECRETARY. *[Name]* was appointed chairperson of the meeting, and *[Name]* was appointed as secretary to prepare a record of the proceedings.

3. ELECTION OF DIRECTORS. The following persons were elected as directors for the terms provided in the bylaws:

Name:

Address:

Term: *[e.g., one year]*

[Add additional names as applicable].

4. ELECTION OF OFFICERS. The following officers were elected:

Name:

Address:

Office: *[e.g., President]*

[Add additional names as applicable].

5. APPROVAL OF ACTIONS SECTION. The actions and undertakings of the directors, officers, employees, and agents of the corporation were approved with respect to: *[Specify, e.g.: "All actions subsequent to the last meeting of the Board of Directors and Shareholders"].*

6. FINANCIAL STATEMENTS PRESENTATION. The financial statements for the year ending *[Date]*, as prepared by the corporation's accountant(s), were approved.

7. DIVIDENDS. The payment of dividends to the stockholders of record on *[Date]* was approved in accordance with the attached schedule.

8. ESTABLISH BANKING RELATIONSHIP. The officers are authorized to open accounts with *[Name of Bank]* The form of resolution as provided by the bank was adopted and a copy is attached. The attached bank form resolution states the names of the persons who are authorized to sign checks and drafts.

9. AUTHORIZATION OF CORPORATE ACTION. The officers and directors were authorized to take all actions and to sign all documents reasonably needed to:

[Specify, e.g.:

-Establish a group health plan as reflected in the attached explanation.

-Establish a life insurance plan as reflected in the attached explanation.

-Establish a pension plan as reflected in the attached explanation.

-Establish a disability insurance plan as reflected in the attached explanation.]

10. NEXT MEETING. The next meeting of the Board of Directors and Shareholders will be held on *[Date]*, at *[Time]*, at the corporation's place of business.

There being no further business, the meeting was duly adjourned.

BY: _____

[SIGNATURE LINE—SECRETARY]

FORM 3-3

CORPORATE PROXY FOR *[NAME OF CORPORATION]*

I, *[Name of Stockholder]*, the undersigned stockholder (the "Stockholder"), residing at *[Address of Stockholder]*, hereby designates *[Name of Designated Proxy]* (the "Proxy") as my proxy with respect to the my shares of stock (the "Stock") in *[Name of Corporation]* (the "Corporation").

By this designation of proxy, I hereby revoke any prior designation of proxy that I may have given previously with respect to the Stock.

This designation of proxy shall be effective immediately, and shall continue in effect until terminated by a written notice delivered to the Corporation.

The Proxy shall have the full power, as my substitute, to represent the me and vote the Stock on all issues and motions that are properly presented at the meeting(s) for which this designation of proxy is effective.

The Proxy shall have the authority to vote entirely in the discretion of the Proxy.

DATED: BY: _____

                    [SIGNATURE LINE—STOCKHOLDER]

STATE OF   )

                  :ss.:

COUNTY OF   )

On the ___ day of _____, 20__, before me personally came *[Name]*, to me known to be the individual described in and who executed the foregoing instrument, and acknowledged that he/she executed the same.

_____
   [NOTARY PUBLIC]

FORM 3-4

NOTICE OF A MEETING OF THE BOARD OF DIRECTORS AND SHAREHOLDERS OF *[NAME OF CORPORATION]*

Date: *[Date]*

To: The Directors and Shareholders

You are hereby notified that the Regular meeting of the Board of Directors and Shareholders of the above corporation will be held on *[Date]* at *[Time]*, at the corporation's place of business.

The purpose of the meeting is *[Specify purpose, e.g.: to establish bank accounts]*.

BY: _____
       [SIGNATURE LINE—SECRETARY]

FORM 3-5

PARTNERSHIP AGREEMENT

This Agreement dated July 1, 2001, is by and between John Smith, of 123 Main Street, City, State, 00000, Mary Jones of 321 Central Avenue, City, State 00000, and Jane Doe of 1010 First Avenue, City, State 00000.

The parties agree to carry on business as a partnership, as follows:

ARTICLE ONE: PURPOSE

1. The purpose of the partnership is (state purpose).

ARTICLE TWO: NAME

2. The name of the partnership is Smith, Jones & Doe.

ARTICLE THREE: TERM

3. The partnership will begin as of the date first written above, and will continue indefinitely until terminated.

4. The partnership may be terminated by a majority vote of the partners.

ARTICLE FOUR: CONTRIBUTIONS

5. Each partner will contribute the following property, services or cash to the partnership, as follows:

    a) John Smith—(describe contribution).

    b) Mary Jones—(describe contribution).

    c) Jane Doe—(describe contribution).

ARTICLE FIVE: BANK ACCOUNT

6. The partnership will open and maintain a bank account in the National Bank, located at 456 Main Street, City, State 00000.

7. Check-signing privileges are as follows:

a) Checks under $100.00 may be authorized and signed by any individual partner;

b) Checks from $100.00 to $500.00 require the authorization and signature of two partners;

c) Checks over $500.00 require the authorization and signature of all partners.

ARTICLE SIX: OWNERSHIP

8. The profits and losses of the partnership will be shared by both partners as follows:

a) John Smith—33-1/3%

b) Mary Jones—33-1/3%

c) Jane Doe—33-1/3%

ARTICLE SEVEN: MANAGEMENT

9. All partners will have an equal right to manage the partnership.

10. Partnership decisions will be made by majority vote.

ARTICLE EIGHT: ACCOUNTING

11. The partnership will maintain accounting records at the following location (specify location).

12. Each partner will have the right to inspect such accounting records at any time.

ARTICLE NINE: WITHDRAWAL

13. Upon the withdrawal from the partnership of any partner, or the death of any partner, the partnership will continue and will be managed by the surviving partners.

ARTICLE TEN: PARTNERSHIP INTEREST

14. A partner's interest in the partnership may not be transferred, in whole or in part, to any other party.

15. Upon the withdrawal from the partnership of any partner, or upon the death of any partner, that partner's interest in the partnership shall be sold to the remaining partners, in equal shares, and the remaining

partners will be required to buy that interest, the value of which will be the departing partner's proportionate share of the total value of the partnership.

ARTICLE ELEVEN: WINDING UP

16. Upon termination of the partnership, the partners agree to distribute partnership assets in the following order:

a) Debts of the partnership shall be paid;

b) Income accounts shall be distributed to each partner in his or her proportionate share.

c) Capital accounts shall be distributed to each partner in his or her proportionate share.

d) Any remaining partnership assets shall be distributed to each partner in his or her proportionate share.

ARTICLE TWELVE: MISCELLANEOUS PROVISIONS

17. This agreement contains the entire understanding of the partners.

18. Any modification of this agreement must be in writing and signed by all of the partners.

19. This Agreement is being made in [Name of State] and shall be construed and enforced according to the laws of that state.

20. Additional Terms (specify):

IN WITNESS WHEREOF, the parties have duly executed this Agreement as of the date first written above.

Signature Line for John Smith, Partner

Signature Line for Mary Jones, Partner

Signature Line for Jane Doe, Partner

FORM 3-6

CERTIFICATE OF INCORPORATION OF [CORPORATE NAME]

It is hereby certified that:

1. The name of the proposed corporation is: [insert name].

2. The office of the corporation is to be located in: [insert address of corporation].

3. This corporation is for the following purposes: [insert specific purposes or use all-inclusive clause as follows] To engage in any lawful activity for which corporations may be organized under the laws of the State of [Name of State]

4. The total number of shares which the corporation shall have the authority to issue is: [insert number of authorized shares].

5. The par value of each share of stock is: [insert value of stock].

In witness whereof, this certificate has been subscribed on [insert date] by the undersigned who affirm that the statements made herein are true under the penalties of perjury.

Signature Line for Incorporator

Address Line for Incorporator

FORM 3-7

SECTION 1244 STOCK DESIGNATION CLAUSE

The Board of Directors have determined that in order to attract investment in the corporation, the corporation shall be organized and managed so that it is a Small Business Corporation" as defined in §1244(c)(1) of the Internal Revenue Code, and so that the shares issued by the corporation are §1244 Stock as defined in §1244(c)(1) of the Internal Revenue Code. Compliance with this section will enable shareholders to treat the loss on the sale or exchange of their shares as an ordinary loss on their personal income tax returns.

It is resolved, that the proper officers of the corporation are authorized to sell and issue common shares in the aggregate amount of money and other property (as a contribution to capital and as paid in surplus), which together with the aggregate amount of common shares outstanding at the time of issuance, does not exceed $1,000,000, and

It is resolved that the sale and issuance of shares shall be conducted in compliance with §1244 of the Internal Revenue Code, so that the corporation and its shareholders may obtain the benefits of §1244 of the Internal Revenue Code, and further

It is resolved that the proper officers of the corporation are directed to maintain such accounting records as are necessary so that any shareholder that experiences a loss on the transfer of common shares of the corporation may determine whether they qualify for ordinary loss deduction treatment on their personal income tax returns.

FORM 3-8

BUSINESS PLAN

COVER PAGE

The cover page should contain the basic information about your company, including the name, address and telephone number of the company, and the contact person. You can also include a space to input the name of the person to whom you are giving a copy of your business plan and the date sent.

PART 1: INVESTOR FUNDS

This section should discuss the type of investment being offered, e.g., stock, etc., and the total percentage of ownership that is being offered. Explain why the company is seeking additional financing, e.g., to increase manufacturing capabilities, to expand its market, etc., and show how those funds will be used. Include sections which explain the risks involved, and the potential return on the investment.

PART 2: ABOUT THE COMPANY

This section summarizes the background and goals of the company. Describe the historical background of your company, including the date of organization, legal structure, and, if incorporated, the date and state of incorporation. Discuss the product or service, and the company's track record, if any, in the particular business. Explain why this company is expected to succeed.

PART 3: ABOUT THE PRODUCT (OR SERVICE)

This section should include a detailed description of the product or service, including the costs involved, such as the costs of research and development, manufacturing, and distribution. Also discuss your pricing plans, the sales projections, and potential profits. Compare and differentiate your product or service from those already available. If your product or service is unique, explain why. Include information concerning the legal status of your product, such as patent and trademark protection.

PART 4: THE MARKET

This section should discuss all aspects of the market for the product or service. Detail the overall size and nature of the market, as well as your targeted market segment. Provide hard statistical data that indicates a growing need for your particular product or service. Discuss why the product or service your company offers will be competitive in the market, and differentiate your product or service from those of other companies in the same type of business. Describe your marketing plan, including the established methods of advertising, distribution, and sales. If your product or service is unique, explain what needs it will fulfill and why it will succeed. In addition, discuss future growth and the possible crossover into new markets.

PART 5: COMPANY MANAGEMENT AND PERSONNEL

This section should list your company's management personnel and supporting staff. Discuss each manager's background, accomplishments and experience, and how they will contribute to the success of the company, and state the level of compensation. If any manager has had prior success in the particular business, point that out as well. This section should also include an organizational chart of the various departments of your company, the key support personnel in each department, and their job descriptions.

PART 6: OWNERSHIP AND CONTROL

This section should discuss ownership and control of the company. Discuss the principal's experience in the particular field and qualifications. If applicable, include a list of the stockholders of your company and how they acquired their equity. If there is a board of directors, list the members and their relevant backgrounds.

PART 8: FINANCIAL ANALYSIS

This section should summarize the company's financial condition, including capital contributions and outstanding debt. Detail the prior use of funds, such as research and development, advertising, manufacturing and distribution costs, and working capital. Include documentation of past performance of the company.

PART 9: RISK ANALYSIS

This section should include an analysis of the risks, including the methods undertaken to reduce such risks. Outline and discuss various financial scenarios, including the worst-case and best-case scenarios.

PART 10: STRATEGIES, OBJECTIVES, AND GOALS

This section should discuss your operating plan, including your specific strategies, objectives, and short-term and long-term goals. Outline the objectives you wish to accomplish at various intervals—e.g., quarterly—and your ultimate goal. Include your financial projections for the next 5 years.

APPENDICES

The appendices may include copies of the newspaper clippings, resumes, statistical data, financial tables, etc., which support the various parts of the plan.

FORM 3-9

APPLICATION FOR BUSINESS LOAN (SBA FORM 4)

		OMB Approval No: 3245-0016 Expiration Date: 9/30/01
	U.S. Small Business Administration **APPLICATION FOR BUSINESS LOAN**	

Individual	Full Address	

Name of Applicant Business	Tax I.D. No. or SSN

Full Street Address of Business	Tel. No. (inc. A/C)

City	County	State	Zip	Number of Employees (Including subsidiaries and affiliates)

Type of Business	Date Business Established	At Time of Application ____
Bank of Business Account and Address		If Loan is Approved ____
		Subsidiaries or Affiliates (Separate for above) ____

Use of Proceeds: (Enter Gross Dollar Amounts Rounded to the Nearest Hundreds)	Loan Requested		Loan Request
Land Acquisition		Payoff SBA Loan	
New Construction/ Expansion Repair		Payoff Bank Loan (Non-SBA Associated)	
Acquisition and/or Repair of Machinery and Equipment		Other Debt Payment (Non SBA Associated)	
Inventory Purchase		All Other	
Working Capital (including Accounts Payable)		Total Loan Requested	
Acquisition of Existing Business		Term of Loan - (Requested Mat.)	____ Yrs.

PREVIOUS SBA OR OTHER FEDERAL GOVERNMENT DEBT: If you or any principals or affiliates have 1) ever requested Government Financing or 2) are delinquent on the repayment of any Federal Debt complete the following:

Name of Agency	Original Amount of Loan	Date of Request	Approved or Declined	Balance	Current or Past Due
	$			$	
	$			$	

ASSISTANCE List the name(s) and occupation of anyone who assisted in the preparation of this form, other than applicant.

Name and Occupation	Address	Total Fees Paid	Fees Due
Name and Occupation	Address	Total Fees Paid	Fees Due

Note: The estimated burden completing this form is 12.0 hours per response. You will not be required to respond to any collection of information unless it displays a currently valid OMB approval number. Comments on the burden should be sent to U.S. Small Business Administration, Chief, AIB, 409 3rd St., S.W., Washington, D.C. 20416 and Desk Office for Small Business Administration, Office of Management and Budget, New Executive Office Building, room 10202 Washington, D.C. 20503. OMB Approval (3245-0016).**PLEASE DO NOT SENDFORMS TO OMB. SUBMIT COMPLETED APPLICATION TO LENDER OF CHOICE**

SBA Form 4 (3-00) Previous Edition Obsolete
This form was electronically produced by Elite Federal Forms, Inc.

Page 1

ALL EXHIBITS MUST BE SIGNED AND DATED BY PERSON SIGNING THIS FORM

BUSINESS INDEBTEDNESS: Furnish the following information on all installment debts, contracts, notes, and mortgages payable. Indicate by an asterisk (*) items to be paid by loan proceeds and reason for paying them (present balance should agree with the latest balance sheet submitted).

To Whom Payable	Original Amount	Original Date	Present Balance	Rate of Interest	Maturity Date	Monthly Payment	Security	Current or Past Due
Acct. #	$		$			$		
Acct. #	$		$			$		
Acct. #	$		$			$		
Acct. #	$		$			$		
Acct. #	$		$			$		

MANAGEMENT (Proprietor, partners, officers, directors, all holders of outstanding stock - 100% of ownership must be shown). Use separate sheet if necessary.

Name and Social Security Number and Position Title	Complete Address	%Owned	*Military Service From To	*Sex
Race*: American Indian/Alaska Native ☐ Black/African-Amer. ☐ Asian ☐ Native Hawaiian/Pacific Islander ☐ White ☐ Ethnicity* Hispanic ☐ Not Hispanic ☐				
Race*: American Indian/Alaska Native ☐ Black/African-Amer. ☐ Asian ☐ Native Hawaiian/Pacific Islander ☐ White ☐ Ethnicity* Hispanic ☐ Not Hispanic ☐				
Race*: American Indian/Alaska Native ☐ Black/African-Amer. ☐ Asian ☐ Native Hawaiian/Pacific Islander ☐ White ☐ Ethnicity* Hispanic ☐ Not Hispanic ☐				
Race*: American Indian/Alaska Native ☐ Black/African-Amer. ☐ Asian ☐ Native Hawaiian/Pacific Islander ☐ White ☐ Ethnicity* Hispanic ☐ Not Hispanic ☐				

*This data is collected for statistical purpose only. It has no bearing on the credit decision to approve or decline this application.

THE FOLLOWING EXHIBITS MUST BE COMPLETED WHERE APPLICABLE. ALL QUESTIONS ANSWERED ARE MADE A PART OF THE APPLICATION.

For Guarantee Loans please provide an original and one copy (Photocopy is Acceptable) of the Application Form, and all Exhibits to the participating lender. For Direct Loans submit one original copy of the application and Exhibits to SBA.

1. Submit SBA Form 912 (Statement of Personal History) for each type of individual that the Form 912 requires.

2. If your collateral consists of (A) Land and Building, (B) Machinery and Equipment, (C) Furniture and Fixtures, (D) Accounts Receivable, (E) Inventory, (F) Other, please provide an itemized list (labeled Exhibit A) that contains serial and identification numbers for all articles that had an Original value of greater than $500. Include a legal description of Real Estate Offered as collateral.

3. Furnish a signed current personal balance sheet (SBA Form 413 may be used for this purpose) for each stockholder (with 20% or greater ownership), partner, officer, and owner. Include the assets and liabilities of the spouse and any close relatives living in the household. Also, include your Social Security Number. The date should be the same as the most recent business financial statement. Label it Exhibit B.

4. Include the financial statements listed below: a,b,c for the last three years; also a,b,c, and d as of the same date, - current within 90 days of filing the application; and statement e, if applicable. Label it Exhibit C (Contact SBA for referral if assistance with preparation is wanted.) All information must be signed and dated.
a. Balance Sheet
b. Profit and Loss Statement (if not available, explain why and substitute Federal income tax forms)
c. Reconciliation of Net Worth
d. Aging of Accounts Receivable and Payable (summary not e. detailed)
   Projection of earnings for at least one year where financial statements for the last three years are unavailable or when

5. Provide a brief history of your company and a paragraph describing the expected benefits it will receive from the loan. Label it Exhibit D.

6. Provide a brief description similar to a resume of the education, technical and business background for all the people listed under Management. Label it Exhibit E.

ALL EXHIBITS MUST BE SIGNED AND DATED BY PERSON SIGNING THIS FORM

AGREEMENTS AND CERTIFICATIONS

7. Submit the names, addresses, tax I.D. number(EIN or SSN), and current personal balance sheet(s) of any co-signers and/or guarantors for the loan who are not otherwise affiliated with the business as Exhibit F.

8. Include a list of any machinery or equipment or other non-real estate assets to be purchased with loan proceeds and the cost of each item as quoted by the seller as Exhibit G. Include the seller's name and address.

9. Have you or any officers of your company ever been involved in bankruptcy or insolvency proceedings? If so, please provide the details as Exhibit H.
If none, check here: [ ]Yes [ ]No

10. Are you or your business involved in any pending lawsuits? If yes, provide the details as Exhibit I.
If none, check here: [ ]Yes [ ]No

11. Do you or your spouse or any member of your household, or anyone who owns, manages or directs your business or their spouses or members of their households work for the Small Business Administration, Small Business Advisory Council, SCORE or ACE, any Federal Agency, or the participating lender? If so, please provide the name and address of the person and the office where employed.] Label this Exhibit J.
If none, check here:

12. Does your business, its owners or majority stockholders own or have a controlling interest in other businesses? If so, please provide their names and the relationship with your company along with a current balance sheet and operating statement for each. This should be Exhibit K.

13. Do you buy from, sell to, or use the services of any concern in which someone in your company has a significant financial interest? If yes, provide details on a separate sheet of paper labeled Exhibit L.

14. If your business is a franchise, include a copy of the franchise agreement and a copy of the FTC disclosure statement supplied to you by the Franchisor. Please include it as Exhibit M.

CONSTRUCTION LOANS ONLY

15. Include as a separate exhibit (Exhibit N) the estimated cost of the project and a statement of the source of any additional funds.

16. Provide copies of preliminary construction plans and specifications. Include them as Exhibit O. Final plans will be required prior to disbursement.

EXPORT LOANS

17. Does your business presently engage in Export Trade?
Check here: [ ]Yes [ ]No

18. Will you be using proceeds from this loan to support your company's exports?
Check here: [ ]Yes [ ]No

19. Would you like information on Exporting?
Check here: [ ]Yes [ ]No

Agreements of non-employment of SBA Personnel: I agree that if SBA approves this loan application I will not, for at least two years, hire as an employee or consultant anyone that was employed by SBA during the one year period prior to the disbursement of the

Certification: I certify: (a) I have not paid anyone connected with the Federal Government for help in getting this loan. I also agree to report to the SBA office of the Inspector General, Washington, DC 20416 any Federal Government employee who offers, in return for any type of compensation, to help get this loan approved.

(b) All information in this application and the Exhibits are true and complete to the best of my knowledge and are submitted to SBA so SBA can decide whether to grant a loan or participate with a lending institution in a loan to me. I agree to pay for or reimburse SBA for the cost of any surveys, title or mortgage examinations, appraisals, credit reports, etc., performed by non-SBA personnel provided I

(c) I understand that I need not pay anybody to deal with SBA. I have read and understand SBA Form 159, which explains SBA policy on representatives and their fees

(d) As consideration for any Management, Technical, and Business Development Assistance that may be provided, I waive all claims against SBA and its consultants.

If you knowingly make a false statement or overvalue a security to obtain a guaranteed loan from SBA, you can be fined up to $10,000 and/or imprisoned for not more than five years under 18 usc 1001; if submitted to a Federally insured institution, under 18 USC 1014 by Imprisonment of not more than twenty years and/or a fine of not more than $1,000,000. I authorize the SBA's Office of Inspector General to request criminal record information about me from criminal justice agencies for the purpose of determining my eligibility for programs authorized by

If Applicant is a proprietor or general partner, sign below:

By: _____

If Applicant is a Corporation, sign below:

_____
Corporate Name and Seal   Date

By: _____
              Signature of President

Attested by: _____
              Signature of Corporate Secretary

SUBMIT COMPLETED APPLICATION TO LENDER OF CHOICE

APPLICANT'S CERTIFICATION

By my signature, I certify that I have read and received a copy of the "STATEMENTS REQUIRED BY LAW AND EXECUTIVE ORDER" which was attached to this application. My signature represents my agreement to comply with the approval of my loan request and to comply, whenever applicable, with the hazard insurance, lead-based paint, civil rights or other limitations in this notice.

Each proprietor, each General Partner, each Limited Partner or Stockholder owning 20% or more, each Guarantor and the spouse of each of these must sign. Each person should sign only once.

Business Name: _____

By: _____   _____
    Signature and Title   Date

Guarantors:

_____   _____
Signature and Title   Date

_____   _____
Signature and Title   Date

_____   _____
Signature and Title   Date

_____   _____
Signature and Title   Date

_____   _____
Signature and Title   Date

_____   _____
Signature and Title   Date

_____   _____
Signature and Title   Date

SBA Form 4 (3-00)Previous Edition Obsolete   Page 4

PLEASE READ DETACH AND RETAIN FOR YOUR RECORDS
STATEMENTS REQUIRED BY LAW AND EXECUTIVE ORDER

Federal executive agencies, including the Small Business Administration (SBA), are required to withhold or limit financial assistance, to impose special conditions on approved loans, to provide special notices to applicants or borrowers and to require special reports and data from borrowers in order to comply with legislation passed by the Congress and Executive Orders issued by the President and by the provisions of various inter-agency agreements. SBA has issued regulations and procedures that implement these laws and executive orders, and they are contained in Parts 112, 113, 116, and 117, Title 13, Code of Federal Regulations Chapter 1, or Standard Operating Procedures.

Freedom of Information Act (5 U.S.C. 552)
This law provides, with some exceptions, that SBA must supply information reflected in agency files and records to a person requesting it. Information about approved loans that will be automatically released includes, among other things, statistics on our loan programs (individual borrowers are not identified in the statistics) and other information such as the names of the borrowers (and their officers, directors, stockholders or partners), the collateral pledged to secure the loan, the amount of the loan, its purpose in general terms and the maturity. Proprietary data on a borrower would not routinely be made available to third parties. All requests under this Act are to be addressed to the nearest SBA office and be identified as a Freedom of Information request.

Right to Financial Privacy Act of 1978 (12 U.S.C. 3401)
This is notice to you as required by the Right of Financial Privacy Act of 1978, of SBA's access rights to financial records held by financial institutions that are or have been doing business with you or your business, including any financial institutions participating in a loan or loan guarantee. The law provides that SBA shall have a right of access to your financial records in connection with its consideration or administration of assistance to you in the form of a Government loan or loan guaranty agreement. SBA is required to provide a certificate of its compliance with the Act to a financial institution in connection with its first request for access to your financial records, after which no further certification is required for subsequent accesses. The law also provides that SBA's access rights continue for the term of any approved loan or loan guaranty agreement. No further notice to you of SBA's access rights is required during the term of any such agreement.

The law also authorizes SBA to transfer to another Government authority any financial records included in an application for a loan, or concerning an approved loan or loan guarantee, as necessary to process, service or foreclose on a loan or loan guarantee or to collect on a defaulted loan or loan guarantee. No other transfer of your financial records to another Government authority will be permitted by SBA except as required or permitted by law.

Flood Disaster Protection Act (42 U.S.C. 4011)
Regulations have been issued by the Federal Insurance Administration (FIA) and by SBA implementing this Act and its amendments. These regulations prohibit SBA from making certain loans in an FIA designated floodplain unless Federal flood insurance is purchased as a condition of the loan. Failure to maintain the required level of flood insurance makes the applicant ineligible for any future financial assistance from SBA under any program, including disaster assistance.

Executive Orders -- Floodplain Management and Wetland Protection (42 F.R. 26951 and 42 F.R. 26961)
The SBA discourages any settlement in or development of a floodplain or a wetland. This statement is to notify all SBA loan applicants that such actions are hazardous to both life and property and should be avoided. The additional cost of flood preventive construction must be considered in addition to the possible loss of all assets and investments in future floods.

Occupational Safety and Health Act (15 U.S.C. 651 et seq.)
This legislation authorizes the Occupational Safety and Health Administration in the Department of Labor to require businesses to modify facilities and procedures to protect employees or pay penalty fees. In some instances the business can be forced to cease operations or be prevented from starting operations in a new facility. Therefore, in some instances SBA may require additional information from an applicant to determine whether the business will be in compliance with OSHA regulations and allowed to operate its facility after the loan is approved and disbursed.

Signing this form as borrower is a certification that the OSA requirements that apply to the borrower's business have been determined and the borrower to the best of its knowledge is in compliance.

Civil Rights Legislation
All businesses receiving SBA financial assistance must agree not to discriminate in any business practice, including employment practices and services to the public, on the basis of categories cited in 13 C.F.R., Parts 112, 113, and 117 of SBA Regulations. This includes making their goods and services available to handicapped clients or customers. All business borrowers will be required to display the "Equal Employment Opportunity Poster" prescribed by SBA.

Equal Credit Opportunity Act (15 U.S.C. 1691)
The Federal Equal Credit Opportunity Act prohibits creditors from discriminating against credit applicants on the basis of race, color, religion, national origin, sex, marital status or age (provided that the applicant has the capacity to enter into a binding contract); because all or part of the applicant's income derives from any public assistance program, or because the applicant has in good faith exercised any right under the Consumer Credit Protection Act. The Federal agency that administers compliance with this law concerning this creditor is the Federal Trade Commission, Equal Credit Opportunity, Washington, D.C. 20580.

Executive Order 11738 -- Environmental Protection (38 C.F.R. 25161)
The Executive Order charges SBA with administering its loan programs in a manner that will result in effective enforcement of the Clean Air Act, the Federal Water Pollution Act and other environmental protection legislation. SBA must, therefore, impose conditions on some loans. By acknowledging receipt of this form and presenting the application, the principals of all small businesses borrowing $100,000 or more in direct funds stipulate to the following:

1. That any facility used, or to be used, by the subject firm is not cited on the EPA list of Violating Facilities.

2. That subject firm will comply with all the requirements of Section 114 of the Clean Air Act (42 U.S.C. 7414) and Section 308 of the Water Act (33 U.S.C 1318) relating to inspection, monitoring, entry, reports and information, as well as all other requirements specified in Section 114 and Section 308 of the respective Acts, and all regulations and guidelines issued thereunder.

3. That subject firm will notify SBA of the receipt of any communication from the Director of the Environmental Protection Agency indicating that a facility utilized, or to be utilized, by subject firm is under consideration to be listed on the EPA List of Violating Facilities.

Debt Collection Act of 1982 Deficit Reduction Act of 1984 (31 U.S.C. 3701 et seq. and other titles)
These laws require SBA to aggressively collect any loan payments which become delinquent. SBA must obtain your taxpayer identification number when you apply for a loan. If you receive a loan, and do not make payments as they come due, SBA may take one or more of the following actions:

- Report the status of your loan(s) to credit bureaus
- Hire a collection agency to collect your loan
- Offset your income tax refund or other amounts due to you from the Federal Government
- Suspend or debar you or your company from doing business with the Federal Government
- Refer your loan to the Department of Justice or other attorneys for litigation
- Foreclose on collateral or take other action permitted in the loan instruments.

Immigration Reform and Control Act of 1986 (Pub. L. 99-603)
If you are an alien who was in this country illegally since before January 1, 1982, you may have been granted lawful temporary resident status by the United States Immigration and Naturalization Service pursuant to the Immigration Reform and Control Act of 1986 (Pub. L. 99-603). For five years from the date you are granted such status, you are not eligible for financial assistance from the SBA in the form of a loan or guaranty under section 7(a) of the Small Business Act unless you are disabled or a Cuban or Haitian entrant. When you sign this document, you are making the certification that the Immigration Reform and Control Act of 1986 does not apply to you, or if it does apply, more than five years have elapsed since you have been granted lawful temporary resident status pursuant to such 1986 legislation.

Lead-Based Paint Poisoning Prevention Act (42 U.S.C. 4821 et seq.)
Borrowers using SBA funds for the construction or rehabilitation of a residential structure are prohibited from using lead-based paint (as defined in SBA regulations) on all interior surfaces, whether accessible or not, and exterior surfaces, such as stairs, decks, porches, railings, windows and doors, which are readily accessible to children under 7 years of age. A "residential structure" is any home, apartment, hotel, motel, orphanage, boarding school, dormitory, day care center, extended care facility, college or other school housing, hospital, group practice or community facility and all other residential or institutional structures where persons reside.

FORM 3-10

FINANCIAL STATEMENT OF DEBTOR (SBA FORM 770)

U.S. SMALL BUSINESS ADMINISTRATION
FINANCIAL STATEMENT OF DEBTOR
(INSERT THE WORD "NONE" WHERE APPLICABLE TO ANY OF THE FOLLOWING ITEMS)

1. NAME	2. DATE OF BIRTH (Month, Day and Year)	
3. ADDRESS (Include ZIP Code)	4. PHONE NO.	5. SOCIAL SEC. NO.
6. OCCUPATION SBA LOAN NUMBER	7. HOW LONG IN PRESENT	
8. EMPLOYER'S NAME ADDRESS (Include ZIP Code)	PHONE NUMBER	

9. MONTHLY INCOME:	10. OTHER EMPLOYERS WITHIN LAST 3 YEARS		
Salary or wages $	Name	Address	Dates of Employment
Commissions $			
Other (state source) $			
Total $			

11. NAME OF SPOUSE	SOCIAL SEC. NO.	12. DATE OF BIRTH (Month, Day and Year)
13. OCCUPATION		14. HOW LONG IN PRESENT
15. SPOUSE'S EMPLOYER (Name)	ADDRESS (Include ZIP Code)	PHONE NUMBER

16. MONTHLY INCOME OF SPOUSE:	17. OTHER EMPLOYERS WITHIN LAST 3 YEARS (Of Spouse)		
Salary or wages $	Name	Address	Dates of Employment
Commissions $			
Other (state source) $			
Total $			

18. OTHER DEPENDENTS: _____ NUMBER

Name	Relationship	Age

23. FIXED MONTHLY EXPENSES: (TO NEAREST DOLLAR)

Rent or House Payment	$
Utilities	$
Food	$
Interest	$
Insurance	$
Debt repayments:	
Household furnishings	$
Personal Loans	$
Automobile	$
Doctors and Dentist	$
Other (Specify)	$
TOTAL FIXED MONTHLY EXPENSES	$

19. TOTAL MONTHLY INCOME OF DEPENDENTS (Except Spouse)
$
20. FOR WHAT PERIOD DID YOU LAST FILE A FEDERAL INCOME TAX RETURN?

21. WHERE WAS TAX RETURN FILED?

22. AMOUNT OF GROSS INCOME REPORTED
$

24. ASSETS: (Fair Market Value)	(SHOW AMOUNTS TO NEAREST	
Cash	$	**LIABILITIES**
Checking accounts: (Show location)		Bills owed (grocery, doctor, lawyer, etc.) $
		Installment debt (car, furniture, clothing, etc.)
Savings Accounts: (Show location)		Taxes owed:
		Income
Cash surrender value of life insurance		Other: (Itemize)
Motor Vehicles:		
Make Year License No.		
		Loans payable (to banks, finance companies, etc.)
Debts owed to you: (Name of debtor)		Judgments you owe (Held by whom?)
Stocks, bonds and other securities: (Itemize)		Small Business Administration
		Loans on Life Insurance
Household furniture and goods		Mortgages on Real Estate
Items Used in Trade or Business		Margin Payable on Securities
Other Personal Property: (Itemize)		Other debts: (Itemize)
Real Estate: (Itemize)		
Other Assets: (Itemize)		Total Liabilities $
TOTAL ASSETS:	$	CONTINGENT LIABILITIES $

SBA FORM 770 (1-87) SOP 50 51 USE 3-85 EDITION UNTIL EXHAUSTED   This form was electronically produced by Elite Federal Forms, Inc.   PAGE 1

25. LOANS PAYABLE: Owed To	Date of Loan	Original Amount	Present Balance	Terms of Repayments	How Secured
		$	$	$	
		$	$	$	
		$	$	$	

26. REAL ESTATE OWNED: (Free & Clear) Address	How Owned (Jointly, individually, etc.)		Present Market Value $

27. REAL ESTATE BEING PURCHASED ON CONTRACT OR MORTGAGE Address	Date acquired	Balance Owed $
	Name of Seller or Mortgagor	
	Purchase Price $	Date Next Cash Payment Due
	Present Market Value $	Amount of Next Cash Payment $

28. LIFE INSURANCE POLICIES: Company	Face Amount	Cash Surrender Value	Outstanding Loans
	$	$	$
	$	$	$
	$	$	$

29. LIST ALL REAL AND PERSONAL PROPERTY OWNED BY SPOUSE AND DEPENDENTS VALUED IN EXCESS OF $200:

30. LIST ALL TRANSFERS OF PROPERTY, INCLUDING CASH (BY LOAN, GIFT, SALE, ETC.), THAT YOU HAVE MADE WITHIN THE LAST THREE YEARS. (LIST ONLY TRANSFERS OF $300 OR OVER.)

Property Transferred	To Whom	Date	Amount
			$
			$
			$

31. ARE YOU A CO-MAKER, GUARANTOR, OR A PARTY IN ANY LAW SUIT OR CLAIM NOW PENDING?
☐ YES　　☐ NO　　IF YES, GIVE DETAILS

32. ARE YOU A TRUSTEE, EXECUTOR, OR ADMINISTRATOR?　☐ YES　☐ NO　IF YES, GIVE DETAILS

33. ARE YOU A BENEFICIARY UNDER A PENDING, OR POSSIBLE, INHERITANCE OR TRUST, PENDING OR ESTABLISHED?　NO ☐　YES ☐
IF YES, GIVE DETAILS

34. WHEN DO YOU FEEL THAT YOU CAN START MAKING PAYMENTS ON YOUR SBA DEBT?	35. HOW MUCH DO YOU FEEL THAT YOU CAN PAY SBA ON A MONTHLY OR PERIODIC BASIS?

With knowledge of the penalties for false statements provided by 18 United States Code 1001 ($10,000 fine and/or five years imprisonment) and with knowledge that this financial statement is submitted by me to affect action by the Government, I certify that all the above statement is true and that it is a complete statement of all my income and assets, real and personal, whether held in my name or by another.

Under the provisions of the Privacy Act, loan applicants are not required to give their social security number. The Small Business Administration, however, uses the social security number to distinguish between people with a similar or the same name. Failure to provide this number may not affect any right, benefit or privilege to which an individual is entitled by law but having the number makes it easier for SBA to more accurately identify to whom adverse credit information applies and to keep accurate loan records.

Any Person concerned with the collection of this information, its voluntariness, disclosure or routine under the Privacy Act may contact the Freedom of Information/Privacy Acts Division, Small Business Administration, 409 3rd St., S.W., Washington, D.C. 20416

SIGNATURE	DATE

NOTE: USE ADDITIONAL SHEETS WHERE SPACE ON THIS FORM IS INSUFFICIENT.

SBA FORM 770 (1-87) SOP 50 51 USE 3-85 EDITION UNTIL EXHAUSTED　　　　　PAGE 2

FORM 3-11

CERTIFICATE OF DISSOLUTION OF CORPORATION

New York State
Department of State
Division of Corporations, State Records
and Uniform Commercial Code
Albany, NY 12231

CERTIFICATE OF DISSOLUTION
OF

_____
(Insert corporate name)

Under Section 1003 of the Business Corporation Law

FIRST: The present name of the corporation is:_____
(If the name of the corporation has been changed, the name under which it was formed is:

_____ .)

SECOND: *(must include month, day and year)* The certificate of incorporation was filed by the Department of State on:_____

THIRD: *(must include number and street)* The name and addresses of each officer and director of the corporation is:

_____
_____
_____
_____
_____
_____
_____
_____
_____

FOURTH: The corporation elects to dissolve.

FIFTH: *(check appropriate box)*

    ☐   The dissolution was authorized at a meeting of shareholders by a vote of two-thirds of all outstanding shares entitled to vote or by the unanimous written consent of the holder(s) of all outstanding shares entitled to vote and the certificate of incorporation does not provide for an alternate manner of authorization.

    ☐   The dissolution was authorized in the manner required by provisions in the certificate of incorporation.

Document must be signed on reverse side.

DOS-1337 (Rev. 8/98)

This document must be signed by an officer, director, attorney-in-fact or duly authorized person.

X_____
    (Signature)

_____
    (Type or print name)

_____
    (Title or capacity of signer)

Filed by: _____
    (Name)

_____
(Mailing address)

_____
(City, State and Zip code)

CERTIFICATE OF DISSOLUTION

OF

Under Section 1003 of the Business Corporation Law

(For office use only)

CHAPTER 4
EMPLOYER/EMPLOYEE RELATIONS

FORM 4-1

EMPLOYMENT AGREEMENT

This Agreement dated July 1, 2001, is by and between ABC COMPANY, 123 Main Street, City, State 00000 (hereinafter Company), and John Smith, 456 Central Avenue, City, State 00000, (hereinafter Employee).

For valuable consideration, Company and Independent Contractor agree as follows:

ARTICLE ONE: TITLE

1. Company hereby engages the services of Employee as its (specify title).

ARTICLE TWO: TERM

2. Employee hereby agrees to perform services for Company in the capacity of (title), for a one-year term beginning July 1, 2001 and ending July 1, 2002.

3. This agreement may be renewed annually, for one additional year, on the same terms and conditions as contained herein, unless either party notifies the other prior to the end of the existing term, of that party's intention not to renew this agreement.

ARTICLE THREE: COMPENSATION

4. Company agrees to compensate Employee as follows:

   a) For the first year during which this agreement is in effect, Company agrees to compensate Employee for services rendered at an annual salary of $ _____.

   b) For the second year, and all succeeding years, during which this agreement is in effect, Employee shall receive an increase to Employee's then annual salary of twenty percent (20%).

   c) In addition to Employee's annual salary, Employee will be entitled to an annual bonus equal to ten percent (10%) of Employee's then annual salary.

ARTICLE FOUR: JOB DESCRIPTION

5. Employee shall perform the following duties and responsibilities: (Specify duties and responsibilities)

ARTICLE FIVE: PERFORMANCE EVALUATION

6. Employee's performance will be evaluated by management on an annual basis to determine whether Employee's contract shall be renewed for an additional 1-year term. Such evaluation shall take place prior to the expiration to the existing term.

ARTICLE SIX: EMPLOYEE EXPENSE ACCOUNT

7. Company shall pay or reimburse Employee for all ordinary and necessary expenses incurred by Employee in performance of his or her duties under this agreement, upon submission by Employee of the appropriate expense account forms.

ARTICLE SEVEN: INSURANCE

8. Company shall purchase a term life plan insurance policy on the life of the Employee in a policy amount of not less than [Insert $ Amount], and shall pay all premiums due and owing on such policy. Employee shall designate the beneficiary to such policy.

9. Company shall provide Employee with medical and hospital insurance as outlined in Company's employee handbook, a copy of which is attached hereto.

ARTICLE EIGHT: VACATION AND PERSONAL LEAVE

10. Employee shall be entitled to accrue vacation and personal leave time as outlined in Company's employee handbook, a copy of which is attached hereto.

ARTICLE NINE: NOTICES

11. Any notice required to be given under this agreement shall be sent by certified mail, return receipt requested, as follows:

To Company:

ABC Company

123 Main Street

City, State 00000

To Employee:

John Smith

456 Central Avenue

City, State 00000

ARTICLE TEN: ADDITIONAL PROVISIONS

12. The waiver by either party of any term or condition of this agreement shall not constitute a waiver of any other term or condition of this agreement.

13. This agreement contains the entire understanding of the parties.

14. Any modification of this agreement must be in writing and signed by both parties.

15. This Agreement is being made in [Name of State] and shall be construed and enforced according to the laws of that state.

16. Additional Terms (specify):

IN WITNESS WHEREOF, the parties have duly executed this Agreement as of the date first written above.

Signature Line for Employer ABC Company

Signature Line for Employee John Smith

FORM 4-2

EMPLOYEE NON-COMPETITION AGREEMENT

BE IT KNOWN, for good consideration, and as an inducement for *[Name of Employer]* ("Employer") to employ *[Name of Employee]* ("Employee"), Employee hereby agrees to the following terms and conditions:

1. Employee shall not directly or indirectly compete with the business of Employer, its successors and assigns during his/her term of employment.

2. Employee shall not directly or indirectly compete with the business of Employer, its successors and assigns for a period of *[Specify Number of Years]* years following termination of his/her employment.

3. This terms of this non-competition agreement shall apply notwithstanding the cause or reason for termination, and whether such termination was undertaken by Employer or Employee.

4. The terms referring to non-competition as used herein shall mean that Employee shall not own, manage, operate, consult, or be employed in a business substantially similar to, or materially competitive with, the present business of the Employer, or such other business activity in which the Employer may engage during the term of employment.

5. This agreement shall extend only to such geographic areas within which the Employer generally transacts business, and shall extend to the existing customers or accounts of the Employer wheresoever located.

6. Employee acknowledges that Employer shall or may, in reliance on this agreement, provide Employee access to trade secrets, customer data, and other confidential and proprietary information, and that the provisions of this agreement are reasonably necessary to protect the Company and its good will.

7. Upon any breach if the terms of this agreement, Employer shall be entitled to injunctive relief together with money damages at law, including reasonable attorneys' fees.

8. This agreement shall be binding upon and inure to the benefit of the parties, their successors, assigns and personal representatives.

DATED: BY: _____
                               [SIGNATURE LINE—EMPLOYER]

DATED: BY: _____
                               [SIGNATURE LINE—EMPLOYEE]

FORM 4-3

EMPLOYEE NON-DISCLOSURE AGREEMENT

BE IT KNOWN, that I, *[Name of Employee]*, ("Employee") in consideration of my employment with *[Name of Employer]* ("Employer") do hereby agree and acknowledge the following terms and conditions:

1. During the course of his/her employment, there may be disclosed to Employee certain trade secrets or proprietary information of Employer. Said trade secrets may include, but are not limited to the following: *[Specify, e.g.: technical information; techniques, inventions, computer programs, research projects, customer data, etc.]* and other information confidential to Employer.

2. Employee shall not during, or at any time after the termination of my employment with Employer, and notwithstanding the cause of termination, use for Employee or others, or disclose or divulge to others, including future employers, any trade secrets, confidential information, or any other proprietary information of Employer in violation of this agreement.

3. Upon the termination of his/her employment with Employer, all originals and copies of documents and property of Employer, relating in any way to the Employer's business, or in any way obtained by Employee during the course of his/her employment, shall be promptly returned to Employer.

4. Copies, notes or abstracts of the foregoing shall not be retained by Employee.

5. Employer may notify any future or prospective employer or third party of the existence of this agreement, and shall be entitled to full injunctive relief for any breach.

6. This agreement shall be binding upon Employee and his/her personal representatives and successors in interest, and shall inure to the benefit of the Employer, its successors and assigns.

DATED: BY: _____
                     [SIGNATURE LINE—EMPLOYER]

DATED: BY: _____
                     [SIGNATURE LINE—EMPLOYEE]

FORM 4-4

WORK FOR HIRE AGREEMENT

This Agreement is made effective as of this _____ day of _____, 20___, by and between *[Name of Company]*, of *[Address of Company]* , and *[Name of Service Provider]* of *[Address of Service Provider]*.

In this Agreement, the party who is contracting to receive the services shall be referred to as "Company", and the party who will be providing the services shall be referred to as *[Specify, e.g. if the person is being contracted as a writer, refer to the party as "Writer." For the purposes of this agreement, the term service provider is used throughout]*.

1. DESCRIPTION OF SERVICES Beginning on *[Insert Effective Date]*, *[Service Provider]* will provide the following services, (collectively, the "Services"):

[Specify services to be provided, e.g.: writing the screenplay for an existing novel, a copy of which accompanies this agreement.]

2. PAYMENT FOR SERVICES. Company will pay compensation to *[Service Provider]* for the services provided in the amount of *[Dollar Amount ($xxx)]*. This compensation shall be payable *[Specify manner of payment, e.g.: "in a lump sum upon completion of the Services"]*.

3. TERM. This Agreement terminates *[Specify, e.g.: upon completion of the screenplay.]*

4. RELATIONSHIP OF PARTIES. It is understood by the parties that *[Service Provider]* is an independent contractor with respect to Company, and not an employee of Company. Company does not provide fringe benefits, including health insurance benefits, paid vacation, or any other employee benefit, for the benefit of *[Service Provider]*.

5. WORK PRODUCT OWNERSHIP. Any copyrightable works, ideas, inventions, patents, products, or other information(*) (the "Work Product") developed in whole or in part by *[Service Provider]* in connection with the services provided shall be the exclusive property of Company, and *[Service Provider]*, upon request, shall sign all documents necessary to confirm or perfect the exclusive ownership of "Company" to the Work Product. *[*Add or delete types of copyrightable works which may be produced under the agreement as necessary]*.

6. CONFIDENTIALITY. *[Service Provider]* will not at any time or in any manner, either directly or indirectly, use for the personal benefit of *[Service Provider]*, or divulge, disclose, or communicate in any manner any information that is proprietary to Company. *[Service Provider]* will protect such information and treat it as strictly confidential. This provision shall continue to be effective after the termination of this Agreement. Upon termination of this Agreement, *[Service Provider]* will return to Company all records, notes, documentation and other items that were used, created, or controlled by *[Service Provider]* during the term of this Agreement.

7. ENTIRE AGREEMENT. This Agreement contains the entire agreement of the parties, and there are no other promises or conditions in any other agreement whether oral or written.

8. SEVERABILITY. If any provision of this Agreement shall be held to be invalid or unenforceable for any reason, the remaining provisions shall continue to be valid and enforceable. If a court finds that any provision of this Agreement is invalid or unenforceable, but that by limiting such provision it would become valid and enforceable, then such provision shall be deemed to be written, construed, and enforced as so limited.

DATE: BY: _____
                              [SIGNATURE LINE—ASSIGNOR]

DATE: BY: _____
                              [SIGNATURE LINE—ASSIGNEE]

FORM 4-5

EMPLOYMENT ELIGIBILITY VERIFICATION FORM
(INS FORM I-9)

U.S. Department of Justice
Immigration and Naturalization Service

OMB No. 1115-0136
Employment Eligibility Verification

INSTRUCTIONS
PLEASE READ ALL INSTRUCTIONS CAREFULLY BEFORE COMPLETING THIS FORM.

> **Anti-Discrimination Notice.** It is illegal to discriminate against any individual (other than an alien not authorized to work in the U.S.) in hiring, discharging, or recruiting or referring for a fee because of that individual's national origin or citizenship status. It is illegal to discriminate against work eligible individuals. Employers CANNOT specify which document(s) they will accept from an employee. The refusal to hire an individual because of a future expiration date may also constitute illegal discrimination.

Section 1 - Employee. All employees, citizens and noncitizens, hired after November 6, 1986, must complete Section 1 of this form at the time of hire, which is the actual beginning of employment. **The employer is responsible for ensuring that Section 1 is timely and properly completed.**

Preparer/Translator Certification. The Preparer/Translator Certification must be completed if Section 1 is prepared by a person other than the employee. A preparer/translator may be used only when the employee is unable to complete Section 1 on his/her own. However, the employee must still sign Section 1.

Section 2 - Employer. For the purpose of completing this form, the term "employer" includes those recruiters and referrers for a fee who are agricultural associations, agricultural employers or farm labor contractors.

Employers must complete Section 2 by examining evidence of identity and employment eligibility within three (3) business days of the date employment begins. If employees are authorized to work, but are unable to present the required document(s) within three business days, they must present a receipt for the application of the document(s) within three business days and the actual document(s) within ninety (90) days. However, if employers hire individuals for a duration of less than three business days, Section 2 must be completed at the time employment begins. **Employers must record:** 1) document title; 2) issuing authority; 3) document number, 4) expiration date, if any; and 5) the date employment begins. Employers must sign and date the certification. Employees must present original documents. Employers may, but are not required to, photocopy the document(s) presented. These photocopies may only be used for the verification process and must be retained with the I-9. **However, employers are still responsible for completing the I-9.**

Section 3 - Updating and Reverification. Employers must complete Section 3 when updating and/or reverifying the I-9. Employers must reverify employment eligibility of their employees on or before the expiration date recorded in Section 1. Employers CANNOT specify which document(s) they will accept from an employee.

- If an employee's name has changed at the time this form is being updated/ reverified, complete Block A.

- If an employee is rehired within three (3) years of the date this form was originally completed and the employee is still eligible to be employed on the same basis as previously indicated on this form (updating), complete Block B and the signature block.

- If an employee is rehired within three (3) years of the date this form was originally completed and the employee's work authorization has expired or if a current employee's work authorization is about to expire (reverification), complete Block B and:
    - examine any document that reflects that the employee is authorized to work in the U.S. (see List A or C).
    - record the document title, document number and expiration date (if any) in Block C, and complete the signature block.

Photocopying and Retaining Form I-9. A blank I-9 may be reproduced, provided both sides are copied. The Instructions must be available to all employees completing this form. Employers must retain completed I-9s for three (3) years after the date of hire or one (1) year after the date employment ends, whichever is later.

For more detailed information, you may refer to the INS Handbook for Employers, (Form M-274). You may obtain the handbook at your local INS office.

Privacy Act Notice. The authority for collecting this information is the Immigration Reform and Control Act of 1986, Pub. L. 99-603 (8 USC 1324a).

This information is for employers to verify the eligibility of individuals for employment to preclude the unlawful hiring, or recruiting or referring for a fee, of aliens who are not authorized to work in the United States.

This information will be used by employers as a record of their basis for determining eligibility of an employee to work in the United States. The form will be kept by the employer and made available for inspection by officials of the U.S. Immigration and Naturalization Service, the Department of Labor and the Office of Special Counsel for Immigration Related Unfair Employment Practices.

Submission of the information required in this form is voluntary. However, an individual may not begin employment unless this form is completed, since employers are subject to civil or criminal penalties if they do not comply with the Immigration Reform and Control Act of 1986.

Reporting Burden. We try to create forms and instructions that are accurate, can be easily understood and which impose the least possible burden on you to provide us with information. Often this is difficult because some immigration laws are very complex. Accordingly, the reporting burden for this collection of information is computed as follows: 1) learning about this form, 5 minutes; 2) completing the form, 5 minutes; and 3) assembling and filing (recordkeeping) the form, 5 minutes, for an average of 15 minutes per response. If you have comments regarding the accuracy of this burden estimate, or suggestions for making this form simpler, you can write to the Immigration and Naturalization Service, HQPDI, 425 I Street, N.W., Room 4307r, Washington, DC 20536. OMB No. 1115-0136.

EMPLOYERS MUST RETAIN COMPLETED FORM I-9
PLEASE DO NOT MAIL COMPLETED FORM I-9 TO INS

Form I-9 (Rev. 11-21-91)N

U.S. Department of Justice
Immigration and Naturalization Service

OMB No. 1115-0136
Employment Eligibility Verification

Please read instructions carefully before completing this form. The instructions must be available during completion of this form. **ANTI-DISCRIMINATION NOTICE:** It is illegal to discriminate against work eligible individuals. Employers CANNOT specify which document(s) they will accept from an employee. The refusal to hire an individual because of a future expiration date may also constitute illegal discrimination.

Section 1. Employee Information and Verification. To be completed and signed by employee at the time employment begins.

Print Name: Last	First	Middle Initial	Maiden Name
Address (Street Name and Number)		Apt. #	Date of Birth (month/day/year)
City	State	Zip Code	Social Security #

I am aware that federal law provides for imprisonment and/or fines for false statements or use of false documents in connection with the completion of this form.	I attest, under penalty of perjury, that I am (check one of the following): ☐ A citizen or national of the United States ☐ A Lawful Permanent Resident (Alien # A_____) ☐ An alien authorized to work until ___/___/___ (Alien # or Admission #) _____
Employee's Signature	Date (month/day/year)

Preparer and/or Translator Certification. *(To be completed and signed if Section 1 is prepared by a person other than the employee.) I attest, under penalty of perjury, that I have assisted in the completion of this form and that to the best of my knowledge the information is true and correct.*

Preparer's/Translator's Signature	Print Name
Address (Street Name and Number, City, State, Zip Code)	Date (month/day/year)

Section 2. Employer Review and Verification. To be completed and signed by employer. Examine one document from List A OR examine one document from List B and one from List C, as listed on the reverse of this form, and record the title, number and expiration date, if any, of the document(s)

List A	OR	List B	AND	List C
Document title: _____		_____		_____
Issuing authority: _____		_____		_____
Document #: _____		_____		_____
Expiration Date (if any): ___/___/___		___/___/___		___/___/___
Document #: _____				
Expiration Date (if any): ___/___/___				

CERTIFICATION - I attest, under penalty of perjury, that I have examined the document(s) presented by the above-named employee, that the above-listed document(s) appear to be genuine and to relate to the employee named, that the employee began employment on *(month/day/year)* ___/___/___ and that to the best of my knowledge the employee is eligible to work in the United States. (State employment agencies may omit the date the employee began employment.)

Signature of Employer or Authorized Representative	Print Name	Title
Business or Organization Name	Address (Street Name and Number, City, State, Zip Code)	Date (month/day/year)

Section 3. Updating and Reverification. To be completed and signed by employer.

A. New Name (if applicable)	B. Date of rehire (month/day/year) (if applicable)

C. If employee's previous grant of work authorization has expired, provide the information below for the document that establishes current employment eligibility.

Document Title:_____   Document #: _____   Expiration Date (if any): ___/___/___

I attest, under penalty of perjury, that to the best of my knowledge, this employee is eligible to work in the United States, and if the employee presented document(s), the document(s) I have examined appear to be genuine and to relate to the individual.

Signature of Employer or Authorized Representative	Date (month/day/year)

Form I-9 (Rev. 11-21-91)N Page 2

LISTS OF ACCEPTABLE DOCUMENTS

LIST A		LIST B		LIST C
Documents that Establish Both Identity and Employment Eligibility	**OR**	**Documents that Establish Identity**	**AND**	**Documents that Establish Employment Eligibility**

LIST A — Documents that Establish Both Identity and Employment Eligibility

1. U.S. Passport (unexpired or expired)

2. Certificate of U.S. Citizenship (INS Form N-560 or N-561)

3. Certificate of Naturalization (INS Form N-550 or N-570)

4. Unexpired foreign passport, with I-551 stamp or attached INS Form I-94 indicating unexpired employment authorization

5. Alien Registration Receipt Card with photograph (INS Form I-151 or I-551)

6. Unexpired Temporary Card (INS Form I-688)

7. Unexpired Employment Authorization Card (INS Form I-688A)

8. Unexpired Reentry Permit (INS Form I-327)

9. Unexpired Refugee Travel Document (INS Form I-571)

10. Unexpired Employment Authorization Document issued by the INS which contains a photograph (INS Form I-688B)

LIST B — Documents that Establish Identity

1. Driver's license or ID card issued by a state or outlying possession of the United States provided it contains a photograph or information such as name, date of birth, sex, height, eye color and address

2. ID card issued by federal, state or local government agencies or entities, provided it contains a photograph or information such as name, date of birth, sex, height, eye color and address

3. School ID card with a photograph

4. Voter's registration card

5. U.S. Military card or draft record

6. Military dependent's ID card

7. U.S. Coast Guard Merchant Mariner Card

8. Native American tribal document

9. Driver's license issued by a Canadian government authority

For persons under age 18 who are unable to present a document listed above:

10. School record or report card

11. Clinic, doctor or hospital record

12. Day-care or nursery school record

LIST C — Documents that Establish Employment Eligibility

1. U.S. social security card issued by the Social Security Administration (other than a card stating it is not valid for employment)

2. Certification of Birth Abroad issued by the Department of State (Form FS-545 or Form DS-1350)

3. Original or certified copy of a birth certificate issued by a state, county, municipal authority or outlying possession of the United States bearing an official seal

4. Native American tribal document

5. U.S. Citizen ID Card (INS Form I-197)

6. ID Card for use of Resident Citizen in the United States (INS Form I-179)

7. Unexpired employment authorization document issued by the INS (other then those listed under List A)

Illustrations of many of these documents appear in Part 8 of the Handbook for Employers (M-274)

Form I-9 (Rev. 11-21-91)N Page 3

FORM 4-6

INDEPENDENT CONTRACTOR AGREEMENT

This Agreement dated July 1, 2001, is by and between ABC COMPANY, (Company), and John Smith, (Independent Contractor).

For valuable consideration, Company and Independent Contractor agree as follows:

ARTICLE ONE: SERVICES

1. Contractor agrees to perform the following services for Company: (specify)

ARTICLE TWO: COMPLETION

2. Contractor agrees that the services described in Article One will be commenced on July 1, 2001, and will be completed by August 1, 2001.

ARTICLE THREE: LABOR

3. Contractor agrees to hire and compensate Contractor's own employees to perform services under this contract.

ARTICLE FOUR: MATERIALS

4. Contractor agrees to furnish all materials necessary to perform services under this contract.

ARTICLE FIVE: PAYMENT

5. Company agrees to pay Contractor the total amount of [Insert $ Amount] for Contractor's services under this contract. Such payment shall be made as follows: (specify)

ARTICLE SIX: MISCELLANEOUS PROVISIONS

6. The parties agree that Independent Contractor is not an employee of Company and Contractor shall not represent that he or she is an employee of the Company.

7. Contractor agrees to indemnify and hold Company harmless from any claims or liabilities arising out of the performance of Contractor's services under this contract.

8. This agreement contains the entire understanding of the partners.

9. Any modification of this agreement must be in writing and signed by both parties.

10. This Agreement is being made in [Name of State] and shall be construed and enforced according to the laws of that state.

11. Additional Terms (specify):

IN WITNESS WHEREOF, the parties have duly executed this Agreement as of the date first written above.

Signature Line for ABC Company

Signature Line for Independent Contractor John Smith

CHAPTER 5
ESTATE PLANNING

FORM 5-1

WILL

I, Mary Jones, residing at 545 Main Street, in the Town of White Plains, Westchester County, in the State of New York, declare that this is my will. My Social Security Number is 555-55-5555.

FIRST: I revoke all wills and codicils that I have previously made.

SECOND: As used in this will, the term "specific bequest" refers to all specifically identified property that I give to one or more beneficiaries in this will. The term "residuary estate" refers to the rest of my property not otherwise specifically disposed of by this will or in any other manner. The term "residuary bequest" refers to my residuary estate that I give to one or more beneficiaries in this will.

THIRD: All personal property I give in this will through a specific or residuary bequest is given subject to any purchase-money security interest, and all real property I give in this will through a specific or residuary bequest is given subject to any deed of trust, mortgage, lien, assessment, or real property tax owed on the property. As used in this will, "purchase-money security interest" means any debt secured by collateral that was incurred for the purpose of purchasing that collateral. As used in this will, "non-purchase-money security interest" means any debt that is secured by collateral but which was not incurred for the purpose of purchasing that collateral.

FOURTH: Except for purchase money security interests on personal property passed in this will, and deeds of trust, mortgages, liens, taxes and assessments on real property passed in this will, I instruct my personal representative to pay all debts and expenses, including non-purchase-money secured debts on personal property, if any, owed by my estate as provided for by the laws of New York.

FIFTH: I instruct my personal representative to pay all estate and inheritance taxes, if any, assessed against property in my estate or against my beneficiaries as provided for by the laws of New York.

SIXTH: All the rest, residue and remainder of my estate, both real and personal, of whatsoever kind and nature and wheresoever possessed, or to which I in any way be entitled at the time of my decease, I give, devise and bequeath unto my beloved husband, JOHN JONES, if he survives me, absolutely.

SEVENTH: If my husband, JOHN JONES, shall have predeceased me, then I give, devise and bequeath my entire residuary estate, as aforesaid, unto my first alternate beneficiaries, my children, KATHLEEN JONES, born March 13, 1989; and JEANINE JONES, born November 15, 1981; and any other of my children who may be born after the date that this will is made, in equal shares. If any of my children shall have predeceased me, then I give, devise and bequeath my entire residuary estate, as aforesaid, unto my surviving children, in equal shares. I have not provided for my son, JAMES JONES, born March 27, 1973, in this will, because I have provided for him separately as a beneficiary of a life insurance policy. Notwithstanding the foregoing, if at the time of my decease, it is determined that I have no life insurance policy in effect which names my son, JAMES JONES, as beneficiary, then he is hereby named as an additional first alternate beneficiary under my will, to share equally with my other children named herein as first alternate beneficiaries.

EIGHTH: If my first alternate beneficiaries fail to survive me, I hereby give, devise and bequeath my entire residuary estate, as aforesaid, to my second alternate beneficiaries, in equal shares, as follows: To my father-in-law, CHRISTOPHER JONES, presently residing at 53 Dartmouth Street, Garden City, New York; to my father, ARTHUR SMITH, presently residing at 65-85 162nd Street, Flushing, New York; and to my mother, MARGARET SMITH, presently residing at 35-15 84th Street, Jackson Heights, New York. If any of the aforementioned second alternate beneficiaries shall have predeceased me, then I give, devise and bequeath my entire residuary estate, as aforesaid, unto the surviving second alternate beneficiaries, in equal shares.

NINTH: In the event that any of my children are minors at the time of my decease, I authorize my Personal Representative, as trustee, in his discretion, to retain the possession of the respective portion of such minors and accumulate the income therefrom during such minority, or pay over or apply the whole or any part of such principal and income to such minors, or for their support, maintenance, welfare and education, and the receipt of such payee shall be full acquittance to trustee. Any principal or income so retained or accumulated shall be paid to the minor upon attaining the age of twenty-one (21) years. Nothing herein contained shall be deemed to defer the vesting of any estate or interest in possession or otherwise.

TENTH: In the event that, upon my death, there is no living person who is entitled by law to the custody of my minor child or children, and who is available to assume such custody, I name my brother, MICHAEL SMITH, presently residing at 175 West 87th Street, Apt. 18-E, New York, New York 10024, as legal guardian of such child, to serve without bond.

ELEVENTH: When this will states that a beneficiary must survive me for the purpose of receiving a specific bequest or residuary bequest, he or she must survive me by 45 days. Notwithstanding the foregoing, property left to my spouse shall pass free of this 45-day survivorship requirement.

TWELFTH: Any specific bequest or residuary bequest made in this will to two or more beneficiaries shall be shared equally among them, unless unequal shares are specifically indicated.

THIRTEENTH: I name my husband, JOHN JONES, 545 Main Street, White Plains, New York, as my personal representative, to serve without bond. If this person shall for any reason fail to qualify or cease to act as personal representative, I name my brother, MICHAEL SMITH, 175 West 87th Street, Apt. 18-E, New York, New York 10024, as my personal representative, also to serve without bond.

FOURTEENTH: I direct my personal representative to take all actions legally permissible to have the probate of my will done as simply and as free of court supervision as possible under the laws of the state having jurisdiction over this will, including filing a petition in the appropriate court for the independent administration of my estate.

FIFTEENTH: I hereby grant to my personal representative the following powers, to be exercised as he or she deems to be in the best interests of my estate:

1. To retain property without liability for loss or depreciation resulting from such retention.

2. To dispose of property by public or private sale, or exchange, or otherwise, and receive and administer the proceeds as a part of my estate.

3. To vote stock, to exercise any option or privilege to convert bonds, notes, stocks or other securities belonging to my estate into other bonds, notes, stocks or other securities, and to exercise all other rights and privileges of a person owning similar property.

4. To lease any real property that may at any time form part of my estate.

5. To abandon, adjust, arbitrate, compromise, sue on or defend and otherwise deal with and settle claims in favor of or against my estate.

6. To continue or participate in any business which is a part of my estate, and to effect incorporation, dissolution or other change in the form of organization of the business.

7. To do all other acts which in his or her judgment may be necessary or appropriate for the proper and advantageous management, investment and distribution of my estate.

The foregoing powers, authority and discretion granted to my personal representative are intended to be in addition to the powers, authority and discretion vested in him or her by operation of law by virtue of his or her office, and may be exercised as often as is deemed necessary or advisable, without application to or approval by any court in any jurisdiction.

SIXTEENTH: If any beneficiary under this will in any manner, directly or indirectly, contests or attacks this will or any of its provisions, any share or interest in my estate given to the contesting beneficiary under this will is revoked and shall be disposed of in the same manner as if that contesting beneficiary had failed to survive me and left no living children.

SEVENTEENTH: If my spouse and I should die simultaneously, or under such circumstances as to render it difficult or impossible to determine who predeceased the other, I shall be conclusively presumed to have survived my spouse for purposes of this will.

I, Mary Jones, the testator, sign my name to this instrument, this 1st day of January, 2001. I hereby declare that I sign and execute this instrument as my last will, that I sign it willingly, and that I execute it as my free and voluntary act for the purposes therein expressed. I declare that I am of the age of majority and otherwise legally empowered to make a will, and under no constraint or undue influence. I hereby execute this will in the presence of ELEANOR JACKSON, EILEEN HARRISON and BARBARA CARTER, whom I have requested to act as witnesses.

Signature Line for Testatrix

In our presence, MARY JONES, the Testatrix, executed, published and declared that the foregoing instrument is her will, and in her presence and in the presence of each other we have signed our names below as witnesses this 1st day of January, 2001.

To the best of our knowledge, the testator is of the age of majority or otherwise legally empowered to make a will, is mentally competent, and under no constraint or undue influence.

We declare under penalty of perjury, that the foregoing is true and correct.

Signature Line for Witness #1

Address of Witness #1

Signature Line for Witness #2

Address of Witness #2

Signature Line for Witness #3

Address of Witness #3

FORM 5-2

SELF-PROVING AFFIDAVIT TO WILL

STATE OF [name of state]

COUNTY OF [name of county]

I, the undersigned, an officer authorized to administer oaths, certify that JOHN JONES JR., the testator, and the witnesses, MARY SMITH, JOHN SMITH and JAMES JACKSON, whose names are signed to the attached instrument and whose signatures appear below, having appeared together before me and having first duly affirmed, each then declared to me that:

1. The attached or foregoing instrument is the last will of the testator;

2. The testator willingly and voluntarily declared, signed and executed the will in the presence of the witnesses;

3. The witnesses signed the will upon request by the testator, in the presence and hearing of the testator, and in the presence of each other;

4. To the best knowledge of each witness the testator was, at that time of the signing, of the age of majority and otherwise legally competent to make a will, of sound mind, and under no constraint or undue influence; and

5. Each witness was and is competent, and was then 18 years of age or older.

    Signature Line for Testator

    Signature Line for Witness #1

    Address of Witness #1

    Signature Line for Witness #2

    Address of Witness #2

    Signature Line for Witness #3

    Address of Witness #3

Sworn to and acknowledged before me by the testator, JOHN JONES JR., and by his witnesses, JOHN SMITH, MARY SMITH and JAMES JACKSON, this 1st day of January, 2001.

Notary Public Signature and Seal

FORM 5-3

CODICIL TO A WILL

On January 1, 2001, I, MARY JONES, executed my will in the presence of the following witnesses:

1.   Eleanor Jackson

2.   Eileen Harrison

3.   Barbara Carter

I hereby make this first codicil to my will, as follows:

Whereas in paragraph designated ELEVENTH of my will I appointed my husband, JOHN JONES, as my executor, I now wish to name my father, ARTHUR SMITH, to act as my executor, also to serve without bond.

I hereby execute this codicil on January 1, 2001, in the presence of Eleanor Jackson, Eileen Harrison and Barbara Carter, whom I requested to act as witnesses.

Signature Line for Testatrix

In our presence, MARY JONES, the Testatrix, executed, published and declared that the foregoing instrument is the first codicil to his will, and in his presence and in the presence of each other we have signed our names below as witnesses this 1st day of January, 2001.

Signature Line for Witness #1

Signature Line for Witness #2

Signature Line for Witness #3

FORM 5-4

DURABLE POWER OF ATTORNEY FOR HEALTH CARE

APPOINTMENT made this (enter date).

I, (Name and address), being of sound mind, willfully and voluntarily appoint (name, address, city, state, phone), as my Health Care Agent (hereinafter "Agent") with a Durable Power of Attorney to make any and all health care decisions for me, except to the extent stated otherwise in this document.

EFFECTIVE DATE

This Durable Power of Attorney and Appointment of Health Care Agent shall take effect at such time as I become comatose, incapacitated, or otherwise mentally or physically incapable of giving directions or consent regarding the use of life-sustaining procedures or any other health care measures.

"Health care" in this context means any treatment, service, or procedure utilized to maintain, diagnose, or treat any physical or mental condition.

DETERMINATION OF MEDICAL CONDITION

A determination of incapacity shall be certified by my attending physician and by a second physician who is neither employed by the facility where I am a patient nor associated in practice with my attending physician and who shall be appointed to independently assess and evaluate my capacity by the appropriate administrator of the facility where I am a patient.

AUTHORITY OF HEALTH CARE AGENT

My Agent is authorized, in consultation with my attending physician, to direct the withdrawal or withholding of any life-sustaining procedures, as defined herein, as (he or she) solely in the exercise of (his or her) judgment shall determine are appropriate to give comply with my wishes and desires.

In addition, my Agent by acceptance of this Appointment agrees and is hereby directed to use (his or her) best efforts to make those decisions that I would make in the exercise of my right to refuse treatment and not those that (he or she) or others might believe to be in my best interests.

APPOINTMENT OF ALTERNATE AGENTS

If the person designated as my Agent is unable or unwilling to accept this Appointment, I designate the following persons to serve as my Agent to make health care decisions for me as authorized by this document. They shall serve in the following order:

1. First Alternate Agent: (name, address and telephone)

2. Second Alternate Agent: (name, address and telephone)

DURATION

I understand that this Power of Attorney exists indefinitely unless I define a shorter time herein or execute a revocation. If I am incapacitated at such time as this Power of Attorney expires (if applicable), the authority I have granted my Agent shall continue until such time as I am capable of giving directions regarding my health care.

(If applicable:) This power of attorney ends on the following date:

COPIES AND DISTRIBUTION

The original of this document is kept at (address where kept). I have made (#) copies of this document. Numbered and signed copies have been provided to the following individuals or institutions: (List names, addresses and phone numbers of individuals and institutions).

STATEMENT OF WITNESSES

I state this (enter date), under penalty of perjury, that the Declarant has identified (himself or herself) to me and that the Declarant signed or acknowledged this Durable Power of Attorney and Appointment of Health Care Agent in my presence.

I believe the Declarant to be of sound mind, and the Declarant has affirmed (his or her) awareness of the nature of this document and is signing it voluntarily and free from duress. The Declarant requested that I serve as a witness to (his or her) execution of this document.

I am not the person appointed as Agent by this document, and I am not a provider of health or residential care, an employee of a provider of health or residential care, the operator of a community care facility, or an employee of an operator of a health care facility.

I declare that I am not related to the Declarant by blood, marriage, or adoption and that to the best of my knowledge I am not entitled to any part of the estate of the Declarant on the death of the principal under a will or by operation of law.

I declare that I have no claim against any portion of the estate of the Declarant upon (his or her) death, nor any personal financial responsibility for the payment of Declarant's medical bills or any other of Declarant's obligations.

> Signature Line of Witness #1
>
> Address of Witness #1
>
> Signature Line of Witness #2
>
> Address of Witness #2
>
> Signature Line of Witness #3
>
> Address of Witness #3

Subscribed and acknowledged before me by the Declarant, (Name), and by his or her witnesses (Names) on (enter date).

Notary Signature and Stamp

FORM 5-5

FUNERAL SERVICE INSTRUCTIONS

To Whom It May Concern:

Re: Funeral Service and Burial Arrangements

I, *[Name]*, presently residing at *[Address]*, hereby expressly request the following arrangements concerning my funeral service and burial arrangements:

INSERT SPECIFIC REQUESTS, E.G.

1. *[Name of religious affiliation]* be appointed to conduct funeral services at the time of my death. I strictly forbid the appointment of any other individual or institution to serve in this function or capacity.

I further request that my funeral services and burial arrangements be held in the location and manner described below:

Provide details of location and manner in which funeral services are to be held.

Provide details of location and manner in which burial is to take place.

This request shall remain in effect unless expressly revoked by me at a later date, in writing, and notarized.

BY: _____
         [SIGNATURE LINE]

Sworn to and acknowledged before me by *[Name]*, this ____ day of _____ 20___.

_____
[NOTARY PUBLIC]

FORM 5-6

LIFE INSURANCE OWNERSHIP ASSIGNMENT

_____ ("Policy Owner") and _____ ("Transferee") hereby agree as follows:

Policy Owner is the owner of a life insurance policy more fully described as follows: (Describe policy in full detail, including name of company, policy number, etc.).

Policy Owner desires to assign said policy to Transferee as Transferee's sole property.

If there was any consideration or payment by the Transferee to the Policy Owner for the assignment of ownership, describe the consideration paid.

Policy Owner hereby releases and waives all rights to, or incidents of ownership in, the above described insurance policy, including but not limited to:

a) the right to name beneficiaries and to change any existing beneficiaries of the policy;

b) the right to make all payments required by the policy;

c) the right to surrender, cancel or convert the policy.

Dated:

By:_____
        Name of Policy Owner

By:_____
        Name of Transferee

Notary Stamp

FORM 5-7

LIVING WILL

DECLARATION made this ____ day of ____, 2001.

I, (Name and address), being of sound mind, willfully and voluntarily make known my desire that my life shall not be artificially prolonged under the circumstances set forth below, and do hereby declare:

MEDICAL CONDITION

1. If at any time I should have a terminal or incurable condition caused by injury, disease, or illness, certified to be terminal or incurable by at least two physicians, which within reasonable medical judgment would cause my death, and where the application of life-sustaining procedures would serve only to artificially prolong the moment of my death, I direct that such procedures be withheld or withdrawn, and that I be permitted to die with dignity.

2. If at any time I experience irreversible brain injury, or a disease, illness, or condition that results in my being in a permanent, irreversible vegetative or comatose state, and such injury, disease, illness, or condition would preclude any cognitive, meaningful, or functional future existence, I direct my physicians and any other attending nursing or health care personnel to allow me to die with dignity, even if that requires the withdrawal or withholding of nutrition or hydration and my death will follow such withdrawal or withholding.

LIFE-SUSTAINING PROCEDURES

It is my expressed intent that the term "life-sustaining procedures" shall include not only medical or surgical procedures or interventions that utilize mechanical or other artificial means to sustain, restore, or supplant a vital function, but also shall include the placement, withdrawal, withholding, or maintenance of nasogastric tubes, gastrostomy, intravenous lines, or any other artificial, surgical, or invasive means for nutritional support and/or hydration.

"Life-sustaining procedures" shall not be interpreted to include the administration of medication or the performance of any medical procedure deemed necessary to provide routine care and comfort or alleviate pain.

RIGHT TO REFUSE TREATMENT

It is my intent and expressed desire that this Declaration shall be honored by my family, physicians, nurses, and any other attending health care personnel as the final expression of my constitutional and legal right to refuse medical or surgical treatment and to accept the consequences of such refusal. Any ambiguities, questions, or uncertainties that might arise in the reading, interpretation, or implementation of this Declaration shall be resolved in a manner to give complete expression to my legal right to refuse treatment and shall be construed as clear and convincing evidence of my intentions and desires.

REVOCATION OF PREVIOUSLY EXECUTED DOCUMENTS

I understand the full importance of this Declaration and I am emotionally and mentally competent to make this Declaration, and by my execution, I hereby revoke any previously executed Health Care Declaration.

COPIES AND DISTRIBUTION

The original of this document is kept at (address where kept). I have made (#) copies of this document. Numbered and signed copies have been provided to the following individuals or institutions: (List names, addresses and phone numbers of individuals and institutions).

STATEMENT OF WITNESSES

I state this (enter date), under penalty of perjury, that the Declarant has identified (himself or herself) to me and that the Declarant signed or acknowledged this Health Care Declaration in my presence.

I believe the Declarant to be of sound mind, and the Declarant has affirmed (his or her) awareness of the nature of this document and is signing it voluntarily and free from duress. The Declarant requested that I serve as a witness to (his or her) execution of this document.

I declare that I am not related to the Declarant by blood, marriage, or adoption and that to the best of my knowledge I am not entitled to any part of the estate of the Declarant on the death of the principal under a will or by operation of law.

I am not a provider of health or residential care, an employee of a provider of health or residential care, the operator of a community care facility, or an employee of an operator of a health care facility.

I declare that I have no claim against any portion of the estate of the Declarant upon (his or her) death, nor any personal financial responsibility for the payment of Declarant's medical bills or any other of Declarant's obligations.

Signature Line of Witness #1

Address of Witness #1

Signature Line of Witness #2

Address of Witness #2

Signature Line of Witness #3

Address of Witness #3

Subscribed and acknowledged before me by the Declarant, (Name), and by his or her witnesses (Names) on (enter date).

Notary Signature and Stamp

FORM 5-8

UNIFORM DONOR CARD

I, [insert name of donor], born on [insert date of birth] and presently residing at [insert address of donor], in the hope that I may help others, hereby make this anatomical gift, if medically acceptable, to take effect upon my death. The words and marks below indicate my desires.

I give (check one):

1. _____ Any organs or parts needed;

2._____ The following organs or parts only:

Please specify: _____;

for the purposes of transplantation, therapy, medical research or education;

3. _____ My entire body for anatomical study, if needed.

4._____ The following are my limitations or other requirements concerning the above gift:

Please specify, if any:_____.

Signature of Donor:

Date Signed:

Place Signed:

Witness Name and Signature:

Witness Name and Signature:

FORM 5-9

DO NOT RESUSCITATE ORDER ("DNR ORDER")

Name:

Date of Birth:

DO NOT RESUSCITATE THE PERSON NAMED ABOVE. IF IN CARDIAC ARREST, THE INDIVIDUAL NAMED ABOVE IS TO RECEIVE NO CARDIOPULMONARY RESUSCITATION (CPR), NO ELECTRIC DEFIBRILLATION, NO TRACHEAL INTUBATION, AND NO VENTILATORY ASSISTANCE.

Effective Date:

Physician's Signature:

Print Physician's Name:

CONSENT

I understand that this document is a Do Not Resuscitate Order. I further understand that, in the event of suffering cardiac arrest, I am refusing cardiopulmonary resuscitation in situations where death may be imminent. I make this request knowingly and I am aware of the alternatives. I expressly release, on behalf of myself and my family, all persons who shall in the future attend to my medical care of any and all liability whatsoever for acting in accordance with this request. Furthermore, I direct that these guidelines be enforced even though I may develop a diminished mental capacity in the future. I am aware that I may revoke these instructions at any time by (1) the physical destruction or verbal rescinding of this order by the physician who signed it; or (2) by the physical destruction or verbal rescinding of this order by the person who gave written informed consent to the order, including myself or my legally authorized guardian, agent, or surrogate decision maker.

_____
Authorized Signature

FORM 5-10

PERSONAL REPRESENTATIVE INFORMATION LETTER

Following is an example of some of the information that would be helpful to your personal representative in administering your estate. The details should be included in the instructions you leave for your personal representative and should be reviewed periodically and updated as needed:

1. The location of the original and any copies of your will.

2. The names and addresses of the persons you designate as guardians of your minor children, if applicable.

3. The account numbers for all savings, checking and other bank accounts; your safe deposit box number and the location of your safe deposit box key; and the location and address of the banks and the name of your bank officer at each of the banks.

4. The account numbers for all of your credit card accounts.

5. Your burial instructions and cemetery lot information.

6. Information concerning your life insurance policies and the location of the policies.

7. Information concerning any other insurance you may have which could be used to indemnify your estate against any claims which may be brought against it, such as malpractice, homeowners and automobile insurance.

8. The location and description of personal property which may be in the possession of someone else, such as artwork on loan to a museum.

9. A schedule of personal loans of money or property which you may have made, and which are yet outstanding.

10. The names and addresses of persons who may have information concerning your financial affairs, such as your attorney, accountant, stock broker, etc.

11. Information concerning past employment and pension plan entitlements.

12. Personal documents, such as your birth certificate, social security card, marriage certificate, divorce papers (if applicable), passport, etc.

CHAPTER 6
FINANCIAL MATTERS

FORM 6-1

AGREEMENT TO ASSUME OBLIGATION

BE IT KNOWN, for good consideration, this Agreement is entered into on *[Insert Date]*, between *[Name of Creditor]* ("Creditor"), *[Name of Customer]* ("Customer"), and *[Name of Person Assuming Debt]* (the "Undersigned").

It is hereby acknowledged and agreed that:

1. Customer presently owes Creditor the sum of *[Dollar Amount ($xxx)]* Dollars (the "Debt"), which sum is fully due and payable.

2. The undersigned unconditionally and irrevocably agrees to assume and fully pay said Debt and otherwise guarantee to both Creditor and Customer the prompt payment of said debt on the terms below, and to fully indemnify and save harmless Creditor and Customer from any loss thereto.

3. Said Debt shall be promptly paid in the manner following:

[Set forth details for payment of debt].

4. This agreement shall not constitute a release or discharge of the obligations of Customer to Creditor for the payment of said Debt, provided that so long as the undersigned shall promptly pay the Debt in the manner above described, Creditor shall forebear commencing collection action against Customer.

5. In the event of default of payment, Creditor shall have full rights, jointly and severally, against both Customer and/or undersigned for any balance then owing.

6. This Agreement extends only to the above debt and to no other or greater obligation.

7. This agreement shall be binding upon and inure to the benefit of the parties, their successors, assigns and personal representatives.

BY: _____
[SIGNATURE LINE—CREDITOR]

BY: _____
[SIGNATURE LINE—CUSTOMER]

BY: _____

      [SIGNATURE LINE—PARTY ASSUMING DEBT]

WITNESS:

In the presence of:

BY: _____

      [SIGNATURE LINE—WITNESS]

FORM 6-2

AGREEMENT TO COMPROMISE A DEBT

BE IT KNOWN, for good and valuable consideration, I, *[Name of Creditor]* ("Creditor"), as a creditor of *[Name of Debtor]* ("Debtor"), hereby enter into this agreement to compromise and discharge the indebtedness due from Debtor to Creditor on the following terms and conditions:

[Specify terms and conditions, e.g.: Payment must be made within 15 days of the date of this agreement.]

The Debtor and Creditor acknowledge that the present debt due and owing Creditor is in the amount of *[Dollar Amount ($xxx)]* Dollars.

The parties agree that the undersigned creditor shall accept the sum of *[Dollar Amount ($xxx)]* Dollars as full and total payment on said debt and in complete discharge, release, satisfaction and settlement of all monies presently due, provided the sum herein shall be fully and punctually paid in the following manner: *[Specify manner of payment, e.g., by certified check or money order, etc.]*.

In the event the Debtor fails to fully and punctually pay the compromised amount, Creditor shall have full rights to prosecute Creditor's claim for the full amount of *[Dollar Amount ($xxx)]* Dollars, less credits for payments made.

In the event of default in payment the Debtor agrees to pay all reasonable attorneys' fees and costs of collection.

This agreement shall be binding upon and inure to the benefit of the parties, their successors, assigns and personal representatives.

DATED: BY: _____
[SIGNATURE LINE—DEBTOR]

DATED: BY: _____
[SIGNATURE LINE—CREDITOR]

FORM 6-3

SAMPLE GUARANTY

FOR GOOD AND VALUABLE CONSIDERATION, *[Name of Guarantor]* ("Guarantor"), agrees as follows:

1. Guarantor agrees that he is executing this guaranty as an inducement for *[Name of Lender]* ("Lender") to extend credit to *[Name of Borrower]* ("Borrower").

2. Guarantor unconditionally guarantees to Lender, the full and prompt payment of the following debt(s) owed to Lender by Borrower:

(a) Borrower has entered into a financing agreement with Lender for the purchase of a refrigerator to be paid in six equal monthly installments of *[Dollar Amount ($xxx)]* Dollars per month, beginning on *[Insert Date]*, for a total purchase price of *[Dollar Amount ($xxx)]* Dollars.

3. Guarantor agrees to remain bound on this guaranty notwithstanding any extension, renewal, forbearance, waiver, release, discharge or substitution of any collateral or security for the above referenced debt.

4. Guarantor agrees that in the event of a default by Borrower, Lender may seek payment directly from Guarantor.

5. Guarantor's obligation hereunder is limited to the debt herein described.

6. This guaranty shall be binding upon and inure to the benefit of the parties, their successors and assigns.

DATED: BY:_____
                              [SIGNATURE LINE—GUARANTOR]

FORM 6-4

INSTALLMENT NOTE

FOR VALUE RECEIVED, I, *[Name of Borrower]* ("Borrower"), promise to pay to the order of *[Name of Lender],* ("Lender"), the sum of *[Dollar Amount ($xxx)]* Dollars, together with annual interest of *[xx%]* on any unpaid balance.

Principal with interest, shall be paid in *[#]* installments of installments of *[Dollar Amount ($xxx)]* Dollars each, with the first payment due on the 1st day of *[Month/Year]*, and the same amount will be due on the 1st day of each month thereafter until the entire principal amount of this note and earned interest is fully paid.

All payments shall be first applied to earned interest and the balance to principal. Borrower may prepay this note in whole or in part without penalty.

This note shall be fully payable upon demand of any holder of this note in the event borrower shall default in making any payments due under this note within *[e.g. 30]* days of its due date, or upon the death, bankruptcy or insolvency of borrower.

In the event of default, borrower agrees to pay all reasonable attorneys' fees and costs of collection to the extent permitted by law. All parties to this note waive presentment, demand, protest, and all notices thereto, and agree to remain fully bound notwithstanding any extension, indulgence, modification or release or discharge of any party or collateral under this note.

The terms of this note shall be governed by the laws of the State of *[Name of State]*.

DATED: BY: _____
                          [SIGNATURE LINE—BORROWER]

DATED: BY: _____
                          [SIGNATURE LINE—LENDER]

FORM 6-5

PROMISSORY NOTE

AMOUNT: *[$ Amount of Note]*

DATE: *[Date of Note]*

For value received, the undersigned, *[Name of Promisor]*, ("Promisor") promises to pay to the order of *[Name of Payee]*, ("Payee") at *[Address where payment is to be made]* (or at such other place as the Payee may designate in writing) the sum of *[Dollar Amount ($xxx)]*, with interest from *[Date]*, on the unpaid principal at the rate of *[xx%]* annually, upon the following terms and conditions:

1. Unpaid principal after the Due Date shown below shall accrue interest at a rate of *[xx%]* annually until paid.

2. The unpaid principal shall be payable on demand.

3. All payments on this Note shall be applied first in payment of accrued interest and any remainder in payment of principal.

4. The Promisor promises to pay a late charge of Dollar Amount ($xxx)] for each installment that remains unpaid more than *[# Days]* after its due date. This late charge shall be paid as liquidated damages in lieu of actual damages, and not as a penalty.

5. If any installment is not paid when due, the remaining unpaid balance and accrued interest shall become due immediately at the option of the Payee.

6. The Promisor reserves the right to prepay this Note by making payment in full of the then remaining unpaid principal and accrued interest.

7. If any payment obligation under this Note is not paid when due, the Promisor promises to pay all costs of collection, including reasonable attorney fees, whether or not a lawsuit is commenced as part of the collection process.

8. If any of the following events of default occur, this Note and any other obligations of the Promisor to the Payee, shall become due immediately, without demand or notice:

(a) the failure of the Promisor to pay the principal and any accrued interest in full on or before the Due Date;

(b) the death of the Promisor or Payee;

(c) the filing of bankruptcy proceedings involving the Promisor as a Debtor;

(d) the application for appointment of a receiver for the Promisor;

(e) the making of a general assignment for the benefit of the Promisor's creditors;

(f) the insolvency of the Promisor;

(g) the misrepresentation by the Promisor to the Payee for the purpose of obtaining or extending credit; or

(h) the sale, transfer, assignment, or any other disposition of any assets pledged as security for the payment of this Note.

9. Promisor is required to maintain term life insurance payable to the Payee in an amount sufficient to pay the principal and accrued interest in full in the event of Promisor's death.

10. If any one or more of the provisions of this Note are determined to be unenforceable, in whole or in part, for any reason, the remaining provisions shall remain fully operative.

11. All payments of principal and interest on this Note shall be paid in the legal currency of the United States.

12. Promisor waives presentment for payment, protest, and notice of protest and nonpayment of this Note.

13. No renewal or extension of this Note, delay in enforcing any right of the Payee under this Note, or assignment by Payee of this Note shall affect the liability of the Promisor.

14. All rights of the Payee under this Note are cumulative and may be exercised concurrently or consecutively at the Payee's option.

15. This Note shall be construed in accordance with the laws of the State of *[Name of State]*.

DATED: BY _____
                    [SIGNATURE LINE—PROMISOR]

FORM 6-6

RELEASE OF LIEN

BE IT KNOWN, that *[Name of Lienholder]* ("Lienholder"), of *[Address]*, contracted with *[Name of Contracting Party]* on *[Date of Contract]*, to furnish labor and/or materials for construction on the premises owned by *[Name of Property Owner]*, located at *[Address]*.

On *[Date of Filing]*, the lienholder filed a notice of lien against the above property in the Office of the County Clerk, County of _____, in the State of _____. Said lien was duly recorded in *[Set forth recording information]* of the Lien Records of the County.

In consideration of *[Dollar Amount ($xxx)]* Dollars, receipt of which is acknowledged, lienholder releases the above described property and the owner personally from all liability arising from the labor performed and/or materials furnished by lienholder under the terms of the above-mentioned contract, and authorizes and directs that the above-mentioned lien be discharged of record.

DATED: BY: _____
                              [SIGNATURE LINE—LIENHOLDER]

STATE OF   )

                    ss.:

COUNTY OF   )

On the ___ day of _____, 20___, before me personally came *[Name of Lienholder]*, to me known to be the individual described in and who executed the foregoing instrument, and acknowledged that he/she executed the same.

_____
[NOTARY PUBLIC]

FORM 6-7

SAMPLE CREDITOR DEMAND LETTER

Mr. John Smith
123 Main Street
White Plains, New York

RE: Charge-A-Lot Account Number 032773

Dear Mr. Smith:

We have been retained by Charge-A-Lot, Inc. to collect the amount of Three Hundred ($300.00) Dollars which is outstanding on your account. To avoid further action, please send a check or money order for the full amount immediately.

Unless you notify us within thirty days after receipt of this letter that you dispute the validity of this debt, we will assume the debt is valid. If within that time period you notify us that you dispute the debt, or any portion of it, we will obtain verification of the debt from the creditor and send it to you, and will provide you with the name and address of the original creditor if it differs from the current creditor. This letter is an attempt to collect the debt, and any information contained will be used for that purpose.

If you would like to discuss this claim further, please contact the undersigned.

Very truly yours,

Mary Jones, Collection Supervisor

The Pay Now or Else Debt Collection Agency, Inc.

FORM 6-8

SAMPLE PAYMENT AGREEMENT CONFIRMATION LETTER

Mr. John Smith
123 Main Street
White Plains, New York

RE: Charge-A-Lot Account Number 032773

Dear Mr. Smith:

This letter is being sent to you to confirm your agreement to make payments on the above-referenced account so as to avoid further action being taken against you to collect this debt.

As agreed, the outstanding balance of Three Hundred ($300.00) Dollars will be paid in equal monthly installments of Fifty ($50.00) Dollars, beginning on the first of next month, for the next six months until paid in full.

If this letter accurately states the terms of our agreement, please sign where indicated below and return the letter to me in the enclosed self-addressed stamped envelope.

Very truly yours,

Mary Jones, Collection Supervisor

The Pay Now or Else Debt Collection Agency, Inc.

FORM 6-9

SAMPLE NOTICE TO COLLECTION AGENCY TO CEASE CONTACT

[Date]

BY CERTIFIED MAIL—RETURN RECEIPT REQUESTED

TO: [The Pay Now or Else Debt Collection Agency, Inc.]

RE: Charge-A-Lot Account Number 032773

Dear Sir/Madam:

This letter shall serve as a notice to your company to cease any further contact with me in connection with the above-referenced account. As I am sure you are aware, the law requires you to comply with this request.

I am presently unable to make payments on this account because [state reasons, e.g., illness, layoff, etc.]. I am trying to reorganize my financial situation, and intend to take care of this matter as soon as I am able. Although I have explained my circumstances to your employees, they have continued to employ collection tactics which are illegal. [Give details]. This has caused me a great amount of stress.

I would appreciate your cooperation so as to avoid having to assert my legal rights in a court of law. Thank you.

Very truly yours,

John Smith

cc: Charge-A-Lot, Inc.

cc: The Federal Trade Commission

cc: The Better Business Bureau

FORM 6-10

SAMPLE COMPLAINT FOR DEBT COLLECTION HARASSMENT
UNDER THE FAIR DEBT COLLECTION PRACTICES ACT

[CAPTION]

COMPLAINT

I. INTRODUCTION

This is an action brought by an individual consumer for statutory damages under the Fair Debt Collection Practices Act, 15 U.S.C. Section 1692 et. seq. (hereinafter referred to as the "FDCPA"), resulting from Defendants' violations of the statute by engaging in abusive, deceptive and unfair debt collection practices.

II. JURISDICTION

The jurisdiction of this court to determine this action arises under 15 U.S.C. Section 1692k(d) and 28 U.S.C. Section 1337.

III. PARTIES

The plaintiff, John Smith, is a natural person residing at 123 Main Street, City of White Plains, County of Westchester, State of New York.

The defendant, The Pay Now or Else Debt Collection Agency, Inc. is a corporation with its principal place of business located at 1 Park Avenue, New York, New York. The defendant is engaged in the business of collecting debts on behalf of third parties.

IV. STATEMENT OF FACTS

On or about January 1, 2001, defendant telephoned plaintiff at his place of employment, demanding payment of a debt allegedly due a creditor, Charge-A-Lot, Inc., under Account Number 032773.

The plaintiff advised the defendant that he could not receive telephone calls at his place of employment. Nevertheless, the defendant telephoned the plaintiff three additional times on that same day.

Plaintiff thereafter sent a letter to defendant advising them that he did not want to be contacted concerning collection of this debt, either by telephone or in writing. This letter was sent by certified mail with a return receipt requested.

A copy of plaintiff's letter dated January 3, 2001 is attached as Exhibit A. A copy of the return receipt card signed by a representative of defendant on January 5, 2001 is attached as Exhibit B.

On February 1, 2001, defendant telephoned plaintiff at his home and spoke with his minor child. Defendant used threatening and abusive language to the child, to wit: the defendant stated that the child's father would be sent to jail if he did not pay his bills.

On February 3, 2001, defendant again telephoned plaintiff's place of employment. Plaintiff was not present at the time. Plaintiff's co-worker, Mary Jones, received the telephone call. Defendant conduct was abusive and threatening, as set forth in the affidavit of Mary Jones, attached as Exhibit C.

Defendant's violations of the statute include, but are not limited to the following:

[Specify statutory violations]

As a result of the defendant's violations of the FDCPA, plaintiff has suffered actual damages, including mental distress and medical expenses, and is entitled to an award of statutory damages, legal fees and costs.

WHEREFORE, plaintiff respectfully requests that judgment be entered against defendant as follows:

1. Actual damages;

2. Statutory damages in the amount of One Thousand ($1,000) Dollars per violation as set forth in 15 U.S.C. Section 1692k;

Legal fees and costs as set forth in 15 U.S.C. Section 1692k;

Any additional relief as to this Court appears just and reasonable.

Plaintiff requests a jury trial.

[Date]

By: _____

[Attorney Name/Address/Telephone]

[Verification by plaintiff]

CHAPTER 7
LITIGATION

FORM 7-1

AUTHORIZATION TO RELEASE MEDICAL INFORMATION

TO: _____

Name: _____

Address: _____

_____

RE:

Patient Name: _____

Social Security #: _____ DOB: _____

Patient Address: _____

Dates of Treatment: _____

Comments: _____

You are hereby authorized to furnish and release to my attorney:

      ATTORNEY NAME
      STREET
      CITY, STATE ZIP
      TEL: 000-000 0000
      FAX: 000-000 0000

All of the above-referenced medical records, charts, files, prognoses, reports, and such other information relative to my medical condition and/or treatment at any time provided, to the extent said information is available and within your possession. The foregoing authority shall continue in force until revoked by me, in writing. You are further requested not to disclose information concerning any past or present medical condition to any other person without my express written permission.

Thank you for your cooperation.

DATED: BY:_____

SWORN TO BEFORE ME THIS
DAY OF _____,20___

_____
    [NOTARY PUBLIC]

FORM 7-2

GENERAL RELEASE OF CLAIMS

I, *[Name of Releasor]* ("Releasor"), residing at *[Address]* for the sole consideration of the sum of *[Settlement Amount]* Dollars, and upon receipt thereof, do hereby release, acquit and forever discharge *[Name of Defendant]* ("Releasee"), their successors and assigns, heirs, executors and administrators, of and from all causes of action, claims, demands, damages, costs, loss of services, expenses and judgments, which we now have or may have hereafter because of any matter or thing which may have happened, developed or occurred before the signing of this release.

The words "RELEASOR" and "RELEASEE" includes all releasers and all releasees under this RELEASE.

This RELEASE may not be changed orally.

In Witness Whereof, the RELEASORS have hereunto set their hand and seal on the _____ Day of _____, 20___.

BY: _____

       [SIGNATURE LINE—RELEASOR]

STATE OF   )

             ss.:

COUNTY OF   )

On the ___ Day of _____, 20 ___, before me personally came *[Name of Releasor]*, to me known, and known to me to be the individual described in, and who executed the foregoing RELEASE, and duly acknowledged to me that he/she executed the same.

_____

   [NOTARY PUBLIC]

FORM 7-3

GENERAL RELEASE OF CLAIMS—INFANT

Know all men by these Presents:

That I, *[Name of Parent or Legal Guardian]*, state that I am the *[state relationship to infant, i.e., natural mother/father; legal guardian, etc.]* of *[Name of Infant]*, a minor, residing at *[Address]*.

That I, individually and as *[state relationship to infant]* of said minor, for the sole consideration of the sum of *[Settlement Amount]* Dollars, and upon receipt thereof, do hereby release, acquit and forever discharge *[Name of Defendant(s)]*, their successors and assigns, heirs, executors and administrators, of and from all causes of action, claims, demands, damages, costs, loss of services, expenses and judgments, which we now have or may have hereafter because of any matter or thing which may have happened, developed or occurred before the signing of this release, except for those expressly reserved hereunder.

Further, that this release is in settlement of the claim for *[set forth information identifying claim being settled, e.g. claim number; date of incident, etc.]*.

In Witness Whereof, the RELEASOR has hereunto set RELEASOR's hand and seal on the _____ day of _____, 20___.

BY: _____

[SIGNATURE OF PARENT OR GUARDIAN]

STATE OF   )

               ss.:

COUNTY OF   )

On the _____ day of ____, 20___, before me personally came *[Name of Parent or Guardian]*, to me known, and known to me to be the individual described in, and who executed the foregoing RELEASE, and duly acknowledged to me that s/he executed the same.

_____

[NOTARY PUBLIC]

FORM 7-4

JOINDER AND GUARANTEE AGREEMENT

FOR AND IN CONSIDERATION of *[Name of Attorney]*, ("Attorney") performing legal services on behalf of and extending credit to *[Name of Client]*, ("Client"), we join and guarantee to pay Attorney in full any indebtedness now or hereafter owing to the Attorney, arising out of services provided for by the terms of the Retainer Agreement executed on *[Date of Retainer Agreement]*, a copy of which is attached hereto and by this reference incorporated herein.

The liability of the undersigned *[Name(s) of Persons Guaranteeing Client's Legal Fees]*, ("Guarantor(s)") shall be full and absolute as though the same were parties to the Retainer Agreement.

The guarantors understand and agree as follows:

1. Liability for payment of this debt does not create an attorney-client relationship between Attorney and Guarantor(s).

2. Execution of this joinder and guarantee agreement does not entitle the Guarantor(s) to control of litigation.

3. The Guarantor(s) are not entitled to inspection of Attorney's files or information concerning this case.

4 The Attorney will act and rely upon this agreement in extension of credit on behalf of the Client.

This joinder and guarantee agreement shall be immediately binding upon the Guarantor(s) and shall continue in full force and effect until the Guarantor(s) have given written notice to the Attorney not to extend further credit. Delivery of written notice shall operate to prevent any liability on the part of the Guarantor(s) to future indebtedness, but Guarantor(s) shall remain liable for all indebtedness existing prior to delivery of written notice.

Dated this _____ day of _____, 20___.

BY: _____
[SIGNATURE OF GUARANTOR]

FORM 7-5

NOTICE OF CLAIM AGAINST GOVERNMENTAL ENTITY

[CAPTION OF CASE]

TO:

THE SUPERVISOR OR CLERK OF THE TOWN OF *[NAME OF TOWN]*

SIR:

PLEASE TAKE NOTICE that the claimant herein hereby makes claim and demand against the Town of *[NAME OF TOWN]*, as follows:

1. The name and post-office address of each claimant and of his attorney is:

Claimant's Name and Address:

Attorney's Name and Address:

2. The nature of the claim is for damages suffered by the claimant as a result of the wrongful, careless and negligent acts of the Town of *[NAME OF TOWN]*, its agents, servants and employees, without any contributory negligence on the claimant's part, in that they *[set forth allegations, e.g.: failed to repair two large potholes located on First Street, approximately 15-20 feet from its intersection with Main Street, in the Town of [NAME OF TOWN], County of [NAME OF COUNTY], State of [NAME OF STATE]]*.

3. The time when and the place where such claim arose and the nature of the same are as follows: *[Specify time and place of incident and manner in which accident occurred]*.

4. So far as can be determined at this time, the injuries and damages sustained consist of the following: *[Specify damages sustained as a result of claim]*.

5. This notice is made and served on behalf of said infant in compliance with the provisions of *[Specify applicable law, e.g.: Section 50-e of the General Municipal Law]* and such other laws and statutes as are in the case made and provided.

PLEASE TAKE FURTHER NOTICE that claimant demands payment of said claim, and unless said claim is paid within a reasonable time it is the intention of claimant to commence suit against the Town of *[NAME OF TOWN]*.

DATED: BY: _____

[SIGNATURE LINE—CLAIMANT]

FORM 7-6

RETAINER AGREEMENT—PERSONAL INJURY CLAIM

DATE____this day of _____, 20___, the undersigned, _____ ("Client"), retains and employs _____ ("Attorney") as his/her Attorney to represent him/her with full authorization to do all things necessary to investigate and prosecute his/her claims against any and all responsible parties relating to a personal injury action arising out of *[Specify Details of Claim, e.g. an automobile accident which occurred on or about January 1, 2001]*.

The undersigned agrees to the following terms and conditions:

1. Attorney has agreed to take Client's case on a contingency fee basis. This means that Attorney's legal fees will be paid only if Client receives a monetary judgment or settlement in this matter. Attorney will receive no fee if there is no recovery. The contingency fee in this matter will be one-third of any amount recovered either by settlement or judgment following a trial.

2. In addition, it may be necessary for Attorney to advance certain out-of-pocket expenses during the course of litigation. Client agrees to reimburse Attorney for his pro rata share of expenses advanced on his behalf. Such expenses, if any, shall be subtracted from any sum recovered after the attorney fee is deducted. In the event no recovery is made, Client is still responsible for payment of expenses. A monthly statement will be mailed to Client.

3. Client understands and agrees that Attorney cannot commence work in this matter until this agreement is signed and returned to attorney's office. If Attorney is terminated by Client prior to resolution of this matter, Client agrees to pay all legal fees and costs incurred for services rendered on Client's behalf thus far, at Attorney's hourly rate, unless both Attorney and Client agree, in writing, to other payment arrangements prior to such termination.

4. If it becomes necessary to engage the services of any outside experts, such as accountants, psychologists, medical professionals or other expert witnesses, Client will be notified in advance. If Client agrees that the services of any such experts are required, Client will retain their services and agree to be responsible for the costs of such services. In the event that attorney advances the expert's fees on Client's behalf, Client

agrees to reimburse attorney for this expense and any sum not yet paid will be subtracted from any sum recovered after the Attorney fee is deducted, in the event this matter is settled. A monthly statement of such fees, if any, will be mailed to Client.

5. This agreement does not concern any appellate litigation resulting from this matter. If appellate litigation becomes necessary, and Client wishes to retain Attorney's services, a new retainer agreement will be required prior to Attorney representing Client in such litigation.

6. It is Attorney's policy to keep clients fully advised of the status of their cases. Therefore, Attorney will send Client a copy of all letters, pleadings and other paperwork drafted on Client's behalf. In addition, it is agreed that neither Attorney nor Client will agree to any settlement of this matter without the written consent of the other.

7. By signing below where indicated, Client acknowledges that he/she has received a copy of this retainer letter and has read and agreed to its terms and conditions.

ACCEPTED BY: _____
                  [SIGNATURE LINE—CLIENT]

The above employment is hereby accepted on the terms stated.

ACCEPTED BY: _____
                  [SIGNATURE LINE—ATTORNEY]

FORM 7-7

RETAINER AGREEMENT—GENERAL

DATED this _____ day of _____, 20___, the undersigned, *[Name and Address of Client]* ("Client"), retains and employs *[Name of Attorney]* ("Attorney") as his/her attorney to represent him/her in connection with *[Describe Nature of Representation, e.g. matrimonial matter, contract matter, etc.]*.

Client agrees to pay attorney's fees and costs, pursuant to the following terms and conditions:

1. Legal Fee: Attorney's hourly rate of *[Dollar Amount]* per hour.

2. Costs: Actual out-of-pocket expenses incurred on Client's behalf which may include court filing fees, service of process, postage, copying costs, etc.

3. Client understands and agrees that attorney cannot commence work in this matter until this agreement is signed and returned to attorney's office. If attorney is terminated by client prior to resolution of this matter, client agrees to pay any unpaid legal fees and costs incurred for services rendered on client's behalf.

4. Attorney acknowledges that a payment in the amount of *[Dollar Amount]* accompanies this retainer agreement. This retainer will be placed in Attorney's trust account and Attorney will draw on this retainer as fees are earned and costs are incurred. A statement of Client's account will be mailed on or about the 1st day of each month. Client will be responsible for payment of any fees and costs incurred after the retainer has been depleted. In addition, upon resolution of this matter, any portion of the retainer remaining and unearned will be returned to Client.

5. If it becomes necessary to engage the services of any outside experts, such as accountants, psychologists, medical professionals or other expert witnesses, client will be notified in advance. If client agrees that the services of any such experts are required, Client will retain their services and agree to be responsible for the costs of such services. In the event that attorney advances the expert's fees on Client's behalf, Client agrees to reimburse attorney for this expense and any sum not yet paid will be subtracted from any sum recovered after the Attorney fee is de-

ducted, in the event this matter is settled. A monthly statement of such fees, if any, will be mailed to the Client.

6. It is Attorney's policy to keep clients fully advised of the status of their cases. Therefore, Attorney will send Client a copy of all letters, pleadings and other paperwork drafted on Client's behalf. In addition, it is agreed that neither Attorney nor Client will agree to any settlement of this matter without the written consent of the other.

7. By signing below where indicated, Client acknowledges that he has received a copy of this retainer letter and has read and agreed to its terms and conditions.

ACCEPTED BY: _____
              [SIGNATURE LINE—CLIENT]

The above employment is hereby accepted on the terms stated.

ACCEPTED BY: _____
              [SIGNATURE LINE—ATTORNEY]

FORM 7-8

SETTLEMENT AGREEMENT—GENERAL

This Settlement Agreement ("Agreement") is entered into as of *[Insert Date]*, between *[Name of Plaintiff]*, residing at *[Address of Plaintiff]* ("Plaintiff"), and *[Name of Defendant]*, residing at *[Address of Defendant]* ("Defendant").

1. There is now pending in *[Identify Court]*, a civil action ("Action") numbered *[Insert Index Number or Claim Number Assigned to Action]*, entitled *[Insert Caption of Action, i.e. "John Doe vs. Mary Smith"]*.

Following paragraphs # 2-4 are optional and not necessary in all cases:

2. The Action was commenced on *[Date]*, with the filing of a complaint ("Complaint") in which Plaintiff *[description of relief requested set in complaint]* against Defendant.

3. The Action was based on *[description of allegations set forth in complaint]*.

4. In his/her answer filed *[Date]*, Defendant *[set forth denials/affirmative defenses/counterclaims]*.

5. Both parties warrant that they have had advice of counsel throughout the proceedings and negotiations leading to the preparation and execution of this Agreement, and have read it carefully and understand its terms and consequences. *[Optional: (plaintiff's name) is represented by [counsel name/address]*, and *[defendant's name]* is represented by *[counsel name/address]*.

6. Both sides *[optional: have conducted extensive discovery and on the basis of this discovery and other information available to them]* have concluded that, to avoid the burden and expense of litigation, it is in the best interests of both parties to compromise and settle the above-mentioned Action *[and Counterclaim if applicable]*.

NOW THEREFORE, the parties agree as follows:

7. As used in this Agreement:

(a) "Plaintiff" shall include *[insert plaintiff's name]*, his/her employees, representatives, and agents of any kind, and his heirs, assigns, and successors in interest of any kind.

(b) "Defendant" shall include *[insert defendant's name]*, his/her employees, representatives, and agents of any kind, and his heirs, assigns, and successors in interest of any kind.

(c) "Claims" shall mean all claims, demands, obligations, damages, actions and causes of action of any kind whatever, for any relief whatever, on any basis whatever, whether known or not, whether asserted or not, whether fixed or contingent.

8. In consideration of Defendant's payment of *[Dollar Amount ($xxx)]* and describe any other requirements], and full and timely performance of all undertakings made herein, and other consideration stated below, Plaintiff hereby:

(a) Promises to file within ten business days of execution of this Agreement a request for dismissal of the Action, with prejudice; and

(b) Releases Defendant from all Claims arising from or connected in any way with the occurrences alleged in the Complaint, or which were or could have been raised in the Action.

[If there is a counterclaim, following language may be used:]

9. In consideration of the undertakings made in paragraph 8, and full and timely performance of all other undertakings made herein, and other consideration stated below, Defendant hereby:

(a) Promises to file within ten business days of execution of this Agreement a request for dismissal of the Counterclaim, with prejudice, and

(b) Releases Plaintiff from all claims arising from or connected in any way with the occurrences alleged in the Counterclaim, or which were or could have been raised in the Action.

10. Each party acknowledges that it may not now know fully the number or magnitude of the claims it may have against the other, and that it may suffer some further loss or damage in some way connected with the subject matter of the Action *[or Counterclaim]*, but which is unknown or unanticipated at this time. But each party has taken these risks and possibilities into account and accepts that, nevertheless, this Agreement covers all claims which, although unknown at the time of the execution of this Agreement, may be discovered later. Both parties

expressly waive any right to assert hereafter that any claim was excluded from this Agreement through ignorance, oversight, or error.

11. (a) All claims of either party against the other arising out of the circumstances giving rise to the Action *[or Counterclaim]* merge in this Agreement, and this Agreement may be pleaded as a full and complete bar and defense to, and may be used as a basis for an injunction against, any action, suit, or other proceeding instituted in breach of this Agreement.

(b) Nothing in this Agreement shall abridge the right of either party to enforce this Agreement or seek remedy for breach of any of its terms. I f any action, suit or proceeding is instituted to enforce this Agreement or any of its terms, the prevailing party shall be entitled to recover its costs (whether taxable as such or not); expenses; and reasonable attorneys fees.

(c) Any breach of this Agreement by either party will entitle the nonbreaching party to all available legal and equitable remedies and to reactivate the Action *[or Counterclaim]* as the case may be.

As an alternative to (b) and (c) above, the following provision may be used:]

Any dispute between the parties arising out of this Agreement or any of its terms shall be submitted to binding arbitration governed by the rules of the American Arbitration Association. The prevailing party shall be entitled to recover costs, expenses, reasonable attorney fees, costs of arbitration, and other compensation or relief as the arbitrator shall decide.

12. Each party undertakes the obligations set forth in paragraphs 10 through 30, inclusive, as further consideration for the undertakings and promises of the other party. All promises and undertakings in this Agreement are mutual and provide consideration for each other. all terms of this Agreement are material to the Agreement.

13. This Agreement is the result of a good-faith compromise of disputed claims and shall never at any time or for any purpose be considered an admission of the correctness of the claims advanced by either party, or of liability or responsibility by either party, each of whom continues to deny all liability, disclaim all responsibility, and dispute the factual allegations claimed by the other party.

Following Paragraph #14 is Optional:

14. Each party agrees that the provisions of this Agreement are confidential and shall not be voluntarily disclosed to any third person without the prior written consent of the other party; provided, however, that

its terms may be disclosed with five business days' notice to the other party:

(a) In as limited a manner as possible to persons to whom such disclosure is reasonably necessary for the conduct of the personal or business affairs of the parties (such as attorneys, accountants, or tax authorities);

(b) Where necessary to give effect to the terms of paragraph 12; or

(c) When compelled by a governmental authority of competent jurisdiction;

(d) Provided, that if disclosure is compelled by governmental authority and five days' notice is not possible, then as much notice as possible will be given.

15. *[If applicable]* Each party agrees that, as part of its consideration for its undertakings in this Agreement, the Contract from which this Action arose (referred to in paragraph 3) is rescinded by mutual agreement if it ever existed, and has no more effect that if it had never existed.

Detail any other terms of the Agreement in Paragraphs #16 & #17 below:

16. (a) Defendant shall pay Plaintiff *[Dollar Amount ($xxx)]*, as referred to in *[Paragraph #8]* by cashier's checks payable to: *"[Insert Plaintiff's Name]* and *[Insert Name of Attorney]*, as his/her attorney" according to the following schedule:

[Detail Schedule, as applicable]

(i) *[Dollar Amount ($xxx)]*, upon execution of this Agreement by both parties;

(ii) *[Dollar Amount ($xxx)]*, when counsel for Plaintiff provides counsel for Defendant with a file-stamped copy of the Order dismissing the Action with prejudice; and

(iii) *[Dollar Amount ($xxx)]*, in installments of *[Dollar Amount ($xxx)]*, each on the first business day of each *[specify week, month, year, etc.]* beginning with *[Insert Date]* and ending when the full amount shall have been paid.

If applicable:

(b) Defendant may assign the obligation for the payment of the *[Dollar Amount ($xxx)]*, provided for i n section (a) (iii) to an annuity company or other financial institution, subject to the written approval of Plaintiff, which approval shall not unreasonably be withheld; provided, however, that any such assignment shall include assumption by the financial institution of the conditions specified in paragraph 20.

17. (a) *[Specify any other terms of Agreement]*.

18. Each party shall bear its own costs, expenses, and attorneys fees in the Action.

19. (a) If any payment required under this Agreement is not made in a timely fashion, it may be made within 30 days of the date it is due without constituting a breach of the Agreement, provided that interest will be charged at a rate of 10 percent per year, or the maximum rate permitted by law, whichever is less.

(b) If any payment required under this Agreement is more than 30 days overdue, the Agreement may be declared in breach at the option of Plaintiff.

(c) If the Agreement is declared in breach under section (b) above, the entire amount outstanding shall be paid immediately by Defendant, or the assignee of Defendant's obligation, and judgment may be entered against Defendant, or the assignee of Defendant's obligation, for the full amount, with interest at the maximum rate permitted by law from the date of the breach.

20. It is agreed between the parties that the *[Dollar Amount ($xxx)]* agreed on in compromise settlement of the Action is apportioned as follows:

(a) As a compromise for *[state claim: (% of total)]*; and

(b) As a compromise for *[state claim: (% of total)]*; and

(c) As a compromise for *[state claim: (% of total)]*; and

(d) Each payment shall be apportioned pro rata according to the aforementioned schedule.

21. This Instrument supersedes all previous agreements between the parties, contains the whole of the Agreement between the parties, and may not be modified except in writing.

22. In the event any part of this Agreement should be found invalid, unenforceable, or nonbinding, the remaining portion will remain in force and fully binding.

23. This Agreement was negotiated in *[Insert City and State]*, is entered into and is intended to be performed in the State of *[Insert State]*, and the laws of the State of *[Insert State]* govern its interpretation. The language and terms of this Agreement are to be understood in their ordinary sense (except where they are defined herein) and are not to be in-

terpreted in a technical way so as to deprive any party unfairly of substantive rights.

24. Each party warrants that as of the date of execution of the Agreement it has the sole right and authority to execute this Agreement on its behalf and has not sold, assigned, or otherwise transferred any claim or demand relating to any right surrendered by this Agreement.

25. Each party stipulates that if the facts with respect to which this Agreement is executed should be found hereafter to be different than now believed, the Agreement will remain effective nevertheless; each party expressly accepts and assumes the risk of such possible difference in facts. Neither party is relying on any representation not explicitly set forth herein.

26. The waiver by any party of any breach of any term in this Agreement shall not be construed as a waiver of any subsequent breach.

27. (a) Plaintiff, *[Insert Full Name]*, warrants that he has the legal capacity to enter into this Agreement.

(b) Defendant, *[Insert Full Name]*, warrants that he has the legal capacity to enter into this Agreement.

28. The text of this Agreement is the product of negotiation among both parties and their counsel and is not to be construed as having been prepared by one party or the other.

29. This Agreement may be executed in counterparts and be as valid and binding as if both parties signed the same copy.

30. This Agreement becomes effective when executed by both parties. The parties agree to execute all documents and take all further actions reasonably necessary to accomplish the provisions of this Agreement.

DATED: BY: _____
[PLAINTIFF'S SIGNATURE LINE]

DATED: BY: _____
[DEFENDANT'S SIGNATURE LINE]

FORM 7-9

SETTLEMENT AGREEMENT AND RELEASE OF
CLAIMS—ANOTHER FORM: PERSONAL INJURY ACTION

AGREEMENT made as of the ___ day of _____, 20___, between *[Name and Address of Claimant]* ("Claimant"), and *[Name and Address of Settling Party]* ("ABC Supermarket").

IN CONSIDERATION of the mutual covenants and agreements herein contained, the parties hereto agree as follows:

1. In full, final and complete settlement of any and all claims, as provided hereinbelow, and upon execution of this Agreement by the parties, ABC Supermarket agrees to pay Claimant the total sum of *[Dollar Amount ($xxx)]* Dollars by check, subject to collection.

2. Claimant hereby releases and forever discharges ABC Supermarket, its affiliated organizations, and its officers, directors, trustees, employees, agents, attorneys, successors and heirs, from any and all claims arising out of or in connection with any acts or omissions by ABC Supermarket.

3. Specifically, Claimant releases ABC Supermarket from any and all claims resulting from physical injuries sustained as a result of a slip and fall on the premises of ABC Supermarket.

4. The parties agree to keep the terms of this settlement, and the allegations giving rise to this Agreement, completely confidential, and will not hereinafter disclose any information concerning them to anyone, including any newspaper, magazine, radio or television station, or any other media, or any agents, employees or representatives of such media.

5. This Agreement shall be binding upon, and inure to the benefit of, each of the parties to this Agreement, and upon their respective heirs, administrators, representatives, executors and successors, if any.

6. This Agreement constitutes the entire agreement between the parties hereto and supersedes any and all other agreements, understandings, negotiations, or discussions, either oral or in writing, express or implied between the parties hereto.

7. This Agreement may not be amended, altered, modified or otherwise changed, except in a writing executed by the parties hereto.

IN WITNESS WHEREOF, the parties hereto have caused this agreement to be executed as of the date above set forth.

DATED: BY: _____

                                    [SIGNATURE LINE—CLAIMANT]

DATED: BY: _____

                                    [SIGNATURE LINE—ABC SUPERMARKET]

                      BY ITS OWNER: _____

                                    [NAME OF OWNER]

STATE OF   )

              ss.:

COUNTY OF   )

On the _____ day of _____, 20___, before me personally came *[Name of Claimant]*, to me known to be the individual described in and who executed the foregoing instrument, and acknowledged that he/she executed the same.

_____
[NOTARY PUBLIC]

STATE OF   )

              ss.:

COUNTY OF   )

On the ·_____ day of _____, 20___, before me personally came *[Name of Owner]*, the Owner of ABC Supermarket, to me known to be the individual described in and who executed the foregoing instrument, and acknowledged that he/she executed the same.

_____
[NOTARY PUBLIC]

FORM 7-10

STIPULATION OF DISCONTINUANCE OF ACTION

[CAPTION OF CASE]

The matter in difference in the above entitled action having been amicably adjusted by and between the parties, it is hereby stipulated and agreed that the same be and it is hereby dismissed with/without prejudice as to all defendants and without costs against any party.

DATED: BY: _____
                                [Attorney for Plaintiff/Plaintiff Pro Se]

FORM 7-11

VERIFICATION—CORPORATION (LITIGATION PURPOSES)

STATE OF   )

                  : SS.:

COUNTY OF   )

[NAME], being duly sworn, depose and say:

I am the *[Corporate Title, e.g. President]* of *[Name of Corporation]* and a party in the within action; I have read the foregoing *[Describe Document Being Verified, e.g. Complaint]* and know the contents thereof; the same is true to my own knowledge, except as to the matters therein stated to be alleged on information and belief, and as to those matters I believe it to be true. This verification is made by me because the above party is a corporation and I am an officer thereof. The grounds of my belief as to all matters not stated upon my own knowledge are as follows:

[Specify: e. g., corporate records and documents, etc.]

                    BY: _____
                              [SIGNATURE LINE]

Sworn to before me this _____ day of _____, 20___

_____
    [NOTARY PUBLIC]

FORM 7-12

VERIFICATION—INDIVIDUAL (LITIGATION PURPOSES)

STATE OF   )

             : SS.:

COUNTY OF   )

[NAME OF LITIGANT], being duly sworn, depose and say:

I am the *[Plaintiff/Defendant]* in the within action; I have read the foregoing *[Describe Document Being Verified, e.g. Complaint]* and know the contents thereof; the same is true to my own knowledge, except as to the matters therein stated to be alleged on information and belief, and as to those matters I believe it to be true. The grounds of my belief as to all matters not stated upon my own knowledge are as follows:

[Specify, e.g. personal documents]

                  BY: _____
                              [SIGNATURE LINE]

Sworn to before me this _____ day of _____, 20___

_____
     [NOTARY PUBLIC]

FORM 7-13

SATISFACTION OF JUDGMENT AND RELEASE OF LIEN

BE IT KNOWN, that [Name of Lienholder] ("Lienholder"), of [Address] contracted with [Name of Contracting Party] on [Date of Contract] to furnish labor and/or materials for construction on the premises owned by [Name of Property Owner] located at [Address] .

On [Date of Filing] , the lienholder filed a notice of lien against the above property in the Office of the County Clerk, County of [Name of County] in the State of [Name of State]. Said lien was duly recorded in [Set forth recording information] of the Lien Records of the County.

In consideration of [Dollar Amount ($xxx)]   Dollars, receipt of which is acknowledged, lienholder releases the above described property and the owner personally from all liability arising from the labor performed and/or materials furnished by lienholder under the terms of the above-mentioned contract, and authorizes and directs that the above-mentioned lien be discharged of record.

DATED:

BY:_____
[SIGNATURE LINE—LIENHOLDER]

ACKNOWLEDGEMENT

STATE OF   )

COUNTY OF   )

On the___day of _____ , 20_, before me personally came [Name of Lienholder] , to me known to be the individual described in and who executed the foregoing instrument, and acknowledged that he/she executed the same.

_____
NOTARY PUBLIC

FORM 7-14

SAMPLE PREMISES LIABILITY COMPLAINT

[NAME OF COURT]

[CAPTION OF CASE] [FILE INDEX NUMBER]

COMPLAINT

Plaintiff, by his attorney, [name of attorney], complaining of the defendant, alleges, as follows:

FIRST: Plaintiff is a resident of the City, County and State of New York.

SECOND: Upon information and belief at all times hereinafter mentioned the defendant was and still is a domestic corporation, duly organized and existing under and by virtue of the laws of the State of New York.

THIRD: Upon information and belief at all times hereinafter mentioned the defendant owned a supermarket located at 1 Main Street, New York, New York 10001, in the Borough of Manhattan, City and State of New York.

FOURTH: Upon information and belief, at all times hereinafter mentioned the defendant managed, operated, maintained and controlled those premises.

FIFTH: That the public, and more particularly, the plaintiff, were invited to the premises of the defendant for the purpose of purchasing various grocery items from the defendant.

SIXTH: That on the 27th day of March, 2000, the plaintiff, while lawfully on the above premises, was caused to fall, due to the negligence of the defendant, its agents, servants and/or employees.

SEVENTH: That the defendant, its agents, servants and/or employees were negligent in that they failed to clean a slippery substance from the floor of an aisle in the premises and failed to warn the public, and more particularly, the plaintiff, of the dangerous condition existing on the premises, and in generally being careless and reckless concerning the hazardous condition on the premises.

EIGHTH: Upon information and belief at that time and place defendant had actual knowledge and notice of the dangerous condition existing on the premises or the condition had existed for a sufficient length of time prior to the accident such that the defendant could and should have had such knowledge and notice.

NINTH: That the accident and resulting injuries were due to the negligence of the defendant, its agents, servants and/or employees.

TENTH: That as a result of the negligence of the defendant the plaintiff was rendered sick, sore, lame and disabled and suffered serious and painful injuries in and about his head, body and limbs, and has been informed and believes that he will continue to suffer therefrom for an indefinite period of time in the future and that such injuries may be permanent in nature.

ELEVENTH: That by the reason of the negligence of the defendant, the plaintiff has been damaged in the sum of One Hundred Thousand ($100,000) Dollars.

WHEREFORE, plaintiff demands judgment against defendant in the amount of One Hundred Thousand ($100,000) Dollars; costs and disbursements of this action; and any other relief the Court deems appropriate.

PLEASE TAKE NOTICE, that pursuant to the CPLR, you are required to serve a copy of your answer within 20 days after the service of this Complaint.

Dated:

[Signature Line]

[Name of Attorney]

Attorney for Plaintiff

[Attorney's Address]

[Attorney's Telephone Number]

FORM 7-15

SAMPLE ASSAULT AND BATTERY COMPLAINT

[NAME OF COURT]

[CAPTION OF CASE] [FILE INDEX NUMBER]

COMPLAINT

Plaintiff, by his attorney, [name of attorney], complaining of the defendant, alleges, as follows:

FIRST: Plaintiff is a resident of the City, County and State of New York.

SECOND: Upon information and belief at all times hereinafter mentioned the defendant was and still is a resident of the City, County and State of New York.

THIRD: On or about the 12th day of January, 2000, at approximately 10:00 o'clock in the forenoon of that day, the plaintiff was lawfully and properly waiting for a public bus on the bus stop designated for that purpose located at the intersection of Kissena Boulevard and Jewel Avenue, in the County of Queens, City of New York, State of New York.

FOURTH: At that time, date and location, defendant approached plaintiff and, without provocation, willfully, wantonly, maliciously and recklessly assaulted and beat plaintiff and struck plaintiff in the head, face and neck with a metal object, causing plaintiff to sustain the injuries hereinafter alleged.

FIFTH: Solely by reason of the foregoing, plaintiff became sick, sore, lame, and disabled and remains so, and suffered and still suffers great physical and mental pain, and sustained severe injuries to the head, face and neck, and other injuries, and was obliged to expend large sums of money for medical treatment, and has been informed and believes his injuries are permanent.

SIXTH: By reason of the foregoing, the plaintiff has been damaged in the sum of Two Hundred Fifty ($250,000) Dollars.

WHEREFORE, plaintiff demands judgment against defendant in the amount of Two Hundred Fifty ($250,000) Dollars; costs and disbursements of this action; and any other relief the Court deems appropriate.

PLEASE TAKE NOTICE, that pursuant to the CPLR, you are required to serve a copy of your answer within 20 days after the service of this Complaint.

Dated:

[Signature Line]

[Name of Attorney]

Attorney for Plaintiff

[Attorney's Address]

[Attorney's Telephone Number]

FORM 7-16

SUMMONS IN A CIVIL CASE

AO 440 (Rev. 10/93) Summons in a Civil Action - SDNY WEB 4/99

United States District Court

_____ DISTRICT OF _____

SUMMONS IN A CIVIL CASE

V.   CASE NUMBER:

TO: (Name and address of defendant)

YOU ARE HEREBY SUMMONED and required to serve upon PLAINTIFF'S ATTORNEY (name and address)

an answer to the complaint which is herewith served upon you, within _____ days after service of this summons upon you, exclusive of the day of service. If you fail to do so, judgment by default will be taken against you for the relief demanded in the complaint. You must also file your answer with the Clerk of this Court within a reasonable period of time after service.

_____   _____
CLERK   DATE

_____
(BY) DEPUTY CLERK

AO 440 (Rev. 10/93) Summons In a Civil Action -SDNY WEB 4/99

RETURN OF SERVICE		
Service of the Summons and Complaint was made by me[1]	DATE	
NAME OF SERVER (PRINT)	TITLE	

Check one box below to indicate appropriate method of service

☐ Served personally upon the defendant. Place where served: _____

☐ Left copies thereof at the defendant's dwelling house or usual place of abode with a person of suitable age and discretion then residing therein.
Name of person with whom the summons and complaint were left: _____

☐ Returned unexecuted: _____
_____
_____

☐ Other (specify): _____
_____
_____

STATEMENT OF SERVICE FEES		
TRAVEL	SERVICES	TOTAL

DECLARATION OF SERVER

I declare under penalty of perjury under the laws of the United States of America that the foregoing information contained in the Return of Service and Statement of Service Fees is true and correct.

Executed on _____   _____
            Date   Signature of Server

                                             _____
                                             Address of Server

(1)   As to who may serve a summons see Rule 4 of the Federal Rules of Civil Procedure.

FORM 7-17

SUBPOENA IN A CIVIL CASE

AO 88 (Rev. 1/94) Subpoena in a Civil Case - SDNY WEB 4/99

Issued by the
UNITED STATES DISTRICT COURT

_____ **DISTRICT OF** _____

V.	**SUBPOENA IN A CIVIL CASE** CASE NUMBER: [1]

TO:

☐ YOU ARE COMMANDED to appear in the United States District Court at the place, date, and time specified below to testify in the above case.

PLACE OF TESTIMONY	COURTROOM
	DATE AND TIME

☐ YOU ARE COMMANDED to appear at the place, date, and time specified below to testify at the taking of a deposition in the above case.

PLACE OF DEPOSITION	DATE AND TIME

☐ YOU ARE COMMANDED to produce and permit inspection and copying of the following documents or objects at the place, date, and time specified below (list documents or objects):

PLACE	DATE AND TIME

☐ YOU ARE COMMANDED to permit inspection of the following premises at the date and time specified below.

PREMISES	DATE AND TIME

Any organization not a party to this suit that is subpoenaed for the taking of a deposition shall designate one or more officers, directors, or managing agents, or other persons who consent to testify on its behalf, and may set forth, for each person designated, the matters on which the person will testify. Federal Rules of Civil Procedure, 30(b)(6).

ISSUING OFFICER SIGNATURE AND TITLE (INDICATE IF ATTORNEY FOR PLAINTIFF OR DEFENDANT)	DATE
ISSUING OFFICER'S NAME, ADDRESS AND PHONE NUMBER	

(See Rule 45, Federal Rules of Civil Procedure, Parts C & D on Reverse)

[1] If action is pending in district other than district of issuance, state district under case number.

AO 88 (Rev. 1/94) Subpoena in a Civil Case - SDNY WEB 4/99

PROOF OF SERVICE

	DATE	PLACE
SERVED		

SERVED ON (PRINT NAME)	MANNER OF SERVICE

SERVED BY (PRINT NAME)	TITLE

DECLARATION OF SERVER

I declare under penalty of perjury under the laws of the United States of America that the foregoing information contained in the Proof of Service is true and correct.

Executed on _____
DATE

SIGNATURE OF SERVER

ADDRESS OF SERVER

Rule 45, Federal Rules of Civil Procedure, Parts C & D:

(c) PROTECTION OF PERSONS SUBJECT TO SUBPOENAS.

(1) A party or an attorney responsible for the issuance and service of a subpoena shall take reasonable steps to avoid imposing undue burden or expense on a person subject to that subpoena. The court on behalf of which the subpoena was issued shall enforce this duty and impose upon the party or attorney in breach of this duty an appropriate sanction which may include, but is not limited to, lost earnings and reasonable attorney's fee.

(2) (A) A person commanded to produce and permit inspection and copying of designated books, papers, documents or tangible things, or inspection of premises need not appear in person at the place of production or inspection unless commanded to appear for deposition, hearing or trial.

(B) Subject to paragraph (d)(2) of this rule, a person commanded to produce and permit inspection and copying may, within 14 days after service of subpoena or before the time specified for compliance if such time is less than 14 days after service, serve upon the party or attorney designated in the subpoena written objection to inspection or copying of any or all of the designated materials or of the premises. If objection is made, the party serving the subpoena shall not be entitled to inspect and copy materials or inspect the premises except pursuant to an order of the court by which the subpoena was issued. If objection has been made, the party serving the subpoena may, upon notice to the person commanded to produce, move at any time for an order to compel the production. Such an order to compel production shall protect any person who is not a party or an officer of a party from significant expense resulting from the inspection and copying commanded.

(3) (A) On timely motion, the court by which a subpoena was issued shall quash or modify the subpoena if it

(i) fails to allow reasonable time for compliance,

(ii) requires a person who is not a party or an officer of a party to travel to a place more than 100 miles from the place where that person resides, is employed or regularly transacts business in person, except that,

subject to the provisions of clause (c)(3)(B)(iii) of this rule, such a person may in order to attend trial be commanded to travel from any such place within the state in which the trial is held, or

(iii) requires disclosure of privileged or other protected matter and no exception or waiver applies, or

(iv) subjects a person to undue burden.

(B) If a subpoena

(i) requires disclosure of a trade secret or other confidential research, development, or commercial information, or

(ii) requires disclosure of an unretained expert's opinion or information not describing specific events or occurrences in dispute and resulting from the expert's study made not at the request of any party, or

(iii) requires a person who is not a party or an officer of a party to incur substantial expense to travel more than 100 miles to attend trial, the court may, to protect a person subject to or affected by the subpoena, quash or modify the subpoena, or, if the party in whose behalf the subpoena is issued shows a substantial need for the testimony or material that cannot be otherwise met without undue hardship and assures that the person to whom the subpoena is addressed will be reasonably compensated, the court may order appearance or production only upon specified conditions.

(d) DUTIES IN RESPONDING TO SUBPOENA.

(1) A person responding to a subpoena to produce documents shall produce them as they are kept in the usual course of business or shall organize and label them to correspond with the categories in the demand.

(2) When information subject to a subpoena is withheld on a claim that it is privileged or subject to protection as trial preparation materials, the claim shall be made expressly and shall be supported by a description of the nature of the documents, communications, or things not produced that is sufficient to enable the demanding party to contest the claim.

CHAPTER 8
PERSONAL RELATIONSHIPS

FORM 8-1

COHABITATION AGREEMENT

This Agreement is made and entered into this _____ of _____,20___, in the City of _____, State of ____ by and between *[Name]*, residing at *[Address]*, (hereinafter "Name") and *[Name]*, residing at *[Address]*, (hereinafter "Name")

WITNESSETH:

WHEREAS, the parties to this agreement are unmarried persons who began cohabiting *[alternative language: who intend to cohabit with each other]* on or about _____ of _____, 20___, in the City of _____, State of ____. The parties contemplate that this relationship will continue indefinitely, unless terminated as set forth herein.

WHEREAS, the parties declare at this time that they do not intend to become married to each other. Nevertheless, in the event that the parties do marry, it is their mutual intent that this Agreement be deemed a prenuptial agreement and that its terms be given full force and effect as such. Notwithstanding the foregoing, the parties do not intend this cohabitation to be deemed the creation of a common law marriage in any jurisdiction whatsoever.

WHEREAS, in anticipation of their cohabitation, the parties desire to confirm, by this Agreement, the responsibilities, rights and obligations which each party has declared for the other, to establish ownership rights of separate property of the parties; to provide for partnership property; and to provide for any and all other financial and legal consequences arising out of this cohabitation.

WHEREAS, each party agrees that they have had the opportunity to fully discuss this Agreement between themselves and with counsel of their own choosing. This discussion included full disclosure of all property owned by each party, each party's liabilities and income, and all other matters pertaining to their respective financial circumstances. A copy of a schedule containing financial circumstances of each party is attached hereto as Exhibit A and B. respectively.

NOW, THEREFORE, in consideration of the mutual covenants herein, the parties agree as follows:

1. Consideration: The consideration for this agreement is based upon the mutual promises and waivers herein contained. If the cohabitation intended by this Agreement fails to take place, this Agreement shall be deemed null and void for all purposes. *[Note: It is important to note that an agreement founded solely on a meretricious relationship may be deemed void as against public policy and it is thus important to base this Agreement on the contractual provisions each party is providing the other, based on partnership principles.]*

2. Separate Property: The parties agree to keep, as their separate property, all of their respective property as set forth on Exhibits A and B of this Agreement, and that any property subsequently acquired by gift or inheritance, including any increase of such property and any property acquired in exchange for such property, shall remain separate property.

3. Joint Property: The parties agree that from time to time they may voluntarily acquire joint assets, but no property shall be deemed a joint asset unless it is so designated by the parties, in writing, at the time the joint property is acquired. The writing shall indicate the percentage of interest retained by each party in the joint asset.

4. Income and Expenses: The parties intend that the income of each party shall be shared as joint income of the parties *[alternative language: or shall be the separate property of the party earning such income]*. During the term of their cohabitation, the parties agree to share all living expenses as follows: *[Note: The parties may set forth the specific terms of their arrangement as it pertains to the payment of expenses, the expenses which are considered joint expenses and the expenses which shall remain separate expenses of the parties.]*

5. Support: Each party agrees that neither party shall seek support from the other and each hereby waives any right of support of any kind from the other party subsequent to separation or death of the other party. *[Note: The parties may alternatively agree for a schedule of support of either party, particularly in situations where one party is gainfully employed while assisting the other party with furtherance of his or her education during the period of cohabitation.]*

6. Testamentary Provisions: Notwithstanding the foregoing, the parties agree that nothing herein shall be construed to prevent either party from naming the other as a beneficiary of his or her will, or as a donee through gift. However, this paragraph should not be construed as requiring either party to make a gift or a provision in his or her will for the other party.

7. Specific Responsibilities: The parties intend by this Agreement to share living expenses and household chores on a fair and cooperative basis. *[Note: The parties can provide the specific details of their arrangement in as much detail as desired, however, it should be noted that courts generally will not uphold provisions relating to specific performance of personal services, such as the performance of household chores.]*

8. Birth Control: The parties mutually agree to practice birth control by such methods as may be determined by the parties in consultation with their respective physicians. In the event that notwithstanding the foregoing, a pregnancy shall occur, the decision as to whether the child shall be aborted or born shall be the joint decision of both parties *[alternative language: or the sole decision of the mother, etc.]*.

9. Children: In the event a child is born of this relationship, both parents agree to recognize the child as their legitimate child and agree to assume joint parental responsibility for its support. It is further agreed that the parties shall have joint custody of said child.

10. Cessation of Cohabitation: The cohabitation of the parties may be terminated at any time by either party, in which case each party shall retain his or her own separate property as set forth herein, and the joint property shall be divided on the basis of contribution of each party to said asset as set forth in paragraph 3 above.

11. Waiver of Strict Performance: This Agreement constitutes the entire understanding of the parties and no modification or waiver of its terms shall be valid unless in writing and signed by the parties. This Agreement shall not be subject to modification by any court of law. No waiver of a breach or default of any provision of this Agreement shall be deemed a waiver of any subsequent breach or default.

12. Binding Effect: This Agreement shall be binding upon the parties, the heirs, personal representatives and assigns.

13. Partial Invalidity: In the event that any provision of this Agreement is held to be illegal, invalid, unenforceable, or against public policy, the remaining provisions of the Agreement shall remain valid and enforceable.

14. Situs: This Agreement shall be subject to the law of the State of ____ the residence of *[Name]*.

[Note: The residence of one of the parties to the agreement should be chosen as the state whose law shall apply in case of a dispute.]

15. Social Security Numbers:

(a) *[Name]*:

(b) *[Name]*:

16. Attorneys: The name, address and telephone numbers for the attorneys representing each party are as follows:

(a) Attorney for *[Name]*:

(b) Attorney for *[Name]*:

17. Entire Agreement: This Agreement contains the entire understanding of the parties, and there are no representations, warranties, covenants or undertakings other than those expressly set forth herein.

IN WITNESS WHEREOF, the parties hereto have set their hands and seals the day and year first written above.

BY: _____

[SIGNATURE LINE—PARTY]

BY: _____

[SIGNATURE LINE—PARTY]

STATE OF   )

                    : ss.:

COUNTY OF   )

On the _____ day of _____, 20___, before me personally came *[Name]*, to me known to be the individual described in and who executed the foregoing instrument, and acknowledged that he executed the same.

_____

[NOTARY PUBLIC]

STATE OF   )

                    : ss.:

COUNTY OF   )

On the _____ day of _____, 20___, before me personally came *[Name]*, to me known to be the individual described in and who executed the foregoing instrument, and acknowledged that she executed the same.

_____

[NOTARY PUBLIC]

FORM 8-2

PRENUPTIAL AGREEMENT

This Prenuptial Agreement is made and entered into this _____ of _____, 20___, in the City of ___, State of ___ by and between *[Name of husband-to-be]*, residing at *[Address]*, (hereinafter "Husband") and *[Name of wife-to-be]*, residing at *[Address]*, (hereinafter "Wife")

WITNESSETH:

WHEREAS, the parties to this agreement are unmarried persons who are considering entering into a ceremonial marriage on or about the _____ of _____ 20___, in the City of ___, State of ___.

WHEREAS, each of the parties has *[not]* been previously married. *[Note: If either or both parties have been previously married, provide details, including names and dates of birth of any children of the previous marriage].*

WHEREAS, in anticipation of this marriage, the parties desire to confirm, by this agreement, the rights and obligations which will accrue to them, by reason of this marriage, and to accept the provisions of this agreement, in settlement of all rights and claims arising out of this marriage.

WHEREAS, each party agrees that they have had the opportunity to fully discuss this agreement between themselves and with counsel of their own choosing. This discussion included full disclosure of all property owned by each party, each party's liabilities and income, and all other matters pertaining to their respective financial circumstances. A copy of a schedule containing financial circumstances of each party is attached hereto as Exhibit A and B. respectively.

NOW, THEREFORE, in consideration of the mutual covenants herein, the parties agree as follows:

1. Consideration: The consideration for this agreement is based upon the mutual promises and waivers herein contained, and the marriage which is to be solemnized. If the marriage does not take place, this agreement shall be deemed null and void for all purposes.

2. Separate Property: The parties agree to keep, as their separate property, all of their respective premarital property and any property

subsequently acquired by gift or inheritance, including any increase of such property and any property acquired in exchange for such property.

3. Marital Property: The parties intend that any assets acquired by each or both of them during their marriage, which are not contained in Exhibits A and B of this Agreement, will be considered marital property, and subject to division as marital property.

4. Waivers: If this marriage is terminated by death, or dissolved by legal proceedings, each party hereby waives any rights to alimony, maintenance or spousal support of any kind; to dower or curtesy or homestead rights; and to any statutory rights in the other's estate except for those rights to marital property reserved under paragraph 3 above.

5. Testamentary Provisions: Notwithstanding the provisions of paragraph 4 above, the parties agree that nothing herein shall be construed to prevent either party from naming the other as a beneficiary of his or her will, or as a donee through gift. However, this paragraph should not be construed as requiring either party to make a gift or a provision in his or her will for the other party.

6. Additional Instruments: Each party shall take any and all steps and execute and deliver any and all instruments and documents which may be reasonably required for the purpose of giving full force and effect to the provisions of this Agreement.

7. Waiver of Strict Performance: This Agreement constitutes the entire understanding of the parties and no modification or waiver of its terms shall be valid unless in writing and signed by the parties. This Agreement shall not be subject to modification by any court of law. No waiver of a breach or default of any provision of this Agreement shall be deemed a waiver of any subsequent breach or default.

8. Binding Effect: This Agreement shall be binding upon the parties, the heirs, personal representatives and assigns.

9. Partial Invalidity: In the event that any provision of this Agreement is held to be illegal, invalid, unenforceable, or against public policy, the remaining provisions of the Agreement shall remain valid and enforceable.

10. Situs: This Agreement shall be subject to the law of the State of the residence of *[Husband or Wife]*. *[Note: The residence of one of the parties to the agreement should be chosen as the state whose law shall apply in case of a dispute]*.

11. Social Security Numbers:

(a) Husband

(b) Wife:

12. Attorneys: The name, address and telephone numbers for the attorneys representing each party are as follows:

(a) Attorney for Husband:

(b) Attorney for Wife:

13. Entire Agreement: This Agreement contains the entire understanding of the parties, and there are no representations, warranties, covenants or undertakings other than those expressly set forth herein.

IN WITNESS WHEREOF, the parties hereto have set their hands and seals the day and year first written above.

BY: _____
       [SIGNATURE LINE—HUSBAND]

BY: _____
       [SIGNATURE LINE—WIFE]

STATE OF   )

              ss.:

COUNTY OF   )

On the _____ day of _____, 20___, before me personally came *[Name of Husband]*, to me known to be the individual described in and who executed the foregoing instrument, and acknowledged that he executed the same.

_____
   [NOTARY PUBLIC]

STATE OF   )

              ss.:

COUNTY OF   )

On the _____ day of _____, 20___, before me personally came *[Name of Wife]*, to me known to be the individual described in and who executed the foregoing instrument, and acknowledged that she executed the same.

_____
   [NOTARY PUBLIC]

FORM 8-3

SEPARATION AGREEMENT: SIMPLE FORM—NO CHILDREN

This Agreement is made and entered into this _____ of _____, 19___, in the City of ___, State of ___ by and between *[Name of Husband]*, re-siding at *[Address]*, (hereinafter "Husband") and *[Name of Wife]*, resid-ing at *[Address]*, (hereinafter "Wife")

WITNESSETH:

WHEREAS, the parties to this agreement were duly married to each other on the ___ day of _____, 19___, in the City of ___, State of ___.

WHEREAS, there are no issue of the said marriage and no expected is-sue; and

WHEREAS, certain unhappy and irreconcilable differences have arisen between the parties as a result of which they have separated and are now living separate and apart from each other; and

WHEREAS, the parties desire to confirm their separation and to resolve by agreement all issues and disputes existing between them and to set-tle and resolve all aspects of their respective marital rights and obliga-tions, including but not limited to property, support, maintenance, and counsel fees, as permitted by *[Cite the law of the applicable state]*.

WHEREAS, the parties are represented by attorneys of their own selec-tion as set forth in this Agreement, and each of the said parties having been fully informed by his or her counsel of all legal rights and respon-sibilities and each fully understanding same and the terms and condi-tions set forth in this Agreement;

NOW, THEREFORE, in consideration of the premises and mutual cove-nants and undertakings hereinafter set forth, the parties agree as follows:

ARTICLE I
SEPARATION

1. It is, and shall be, lawful for the parties hereto at all times to live sep-arate and apart from each other and to reside from time to time at such place or places as each of the parties may see fit, and to contract, carry

on and engage in any employment, business, or trade, which either may deem fit, free from control, restraints, or interference, direct or indirect, by the other in all respects, as if such parties were sole and unmarried.

2. Neither of the parties shall interfere with the other or with his or her respective liberty of action or conduct, and each agrees that the other may, at any time and at all times, reside and be in such place or places and with such relatives, friends, and acquaintances, as he or she may choose, and each party agrees that he or she will not molest the other or compel or seek to compel the other party to cohabit or dwell with him or her or institute any proceedings for the restoration of conjugal right, or sue, molest, or trouble any other person for receiving, entertaining, or harboring the other party hereto. Neither party shall directly or indirectly make any statements to each other or to any other persons, which are derogatory of the other party.

ARTICLE II
MARITAL RESIDENCE

1. The parties acknowledge and agree that the marital residence was, and the Wife's primary residence remains, the cooperative apartment located at *[Insert Address]* (the "Marital Residence"). The parties further acknowledge and agree that the Wife is the sole owner of, and holds title to, the Marital Residence, and is the sole tenant on a proprietary lease issued with respect to the Marital Residence.

2. The Wife agrees and warrants that she alone shall be responsible for the care, upkeep, maintenance, mortgage, carrying charges, assessments, and all expenses of every kind and nature in connection with the Marital Residence, including without limitation all payments and obligations with respect to any existing Cooperative loan and any and all obligations or expenses with respect to taxes, water and sewer charges, insurance, utilities, telephone, repairs and maintenance.

ARTICLE III
PERSONAL PROPERTY, BANK ACCOUNTS, HOUSEHOLD
EFFECTS

The parties, having considered the circumstances of their marriage, and the facts set forth in *[Cite the law of the applicable state]*, hereby agree as follows with respect to the division of their marital and personal property, other than realty, including all property presently held in the name of the Husband, all property presently held in the name of the Wife, and all property presently held by either the Husband or the Wife in conjunction with any other person(s), including the Husband and the Wife:

1. The Husband and Wife acknowledge and agree that they have heretofore divided between themselves all items of furniture, furnishings and household effects, formerly or presently located in the Marital Residence.

2. The parties acknowledge and agree that as of the date of this Agreement, there exist no bank, savings, or checking accounts in their joint names. The parties further agree that henceforth they will each maintain such bank accounts as they desire in their own individual names, as separate property, and each shall make no claims upon any account held by the other.

3. The Wife shall have exclusive right, title and interest in her personal clothing and effects, including jewelry, if any. The Husband hereby waives and relinquishes any and all claims to any of the personal property described in this Paragraph and agrees to waive and release any and all claims against the Wife for any interest, of any kind or nature, in any and all property not specifically reserved to the Husband under this Agreement.

4. The Husband shall have exclusive right, title and interest in her personal clothing and effects, including jewelry, if any. The Wife hereby waives and relinquishes any and all claims to any of the personal property described in this Paragraph and agrees to waive and release any and all claims against the Husband for any interest, of any kind or nature, in any and all property not specifically reserved to the Wife under this Agreement.

ARTICLE IV
MAINTENANCE, ALIMONY AND SUPPORT

The parties, having considered their respective financial circumstances, their respective present and future earning capacities, and the relevant factors for spousal support set forth in (the applicable State's domestic relations statutes), hereby agree as follows with respect to alimony, maintenance and support:

1. The Husband neither seeks nor requires any alimony, maintenance or support for himself from the Wife and, therefore, no provision for alimony, maintenance or support for the Husband is made herein. The Husband agrees that he has not claimed, and that he will not hereafter claim against the Wife for support and maintenance.

The Husband hereby expressly waives and releases any and all claims to alimony, maintenance or support from the Wife.

2. The Wife neither seeks nor requires any alimony, maintenance or support for himself from the Husband and, therefore, no provision for alimony' maintenance or support for the Wife is made herein. The Wife agrees that he has not claimed, and that he will not hereafter claim against the Husband for support and maintenance. The Wife hereby expressly waives and releases any and all claims to alimony, maintenance or support from the Husband.

ARTICLE V
INSURANCE

Neither party shall be under any obligation to provide for the other any policy of health insurance, life insurance, or any other form or type of insurance.

ARTICLE VI
INCOME TAXES

1. The parties acknowledge that they have heretofore filed joint income tax returns with the appropriate federal and state taxing authorities. Except as otherwise provided herein, all liabilities on any such joint income tax returns shall be equally borne by the parties, and all refunds on such returns shall be equally divided by the parties. The Husband and Wife each hereby warrant and represent to the other that to the best of his or her knowledge all federal, state and local income tax returns on all joint returns heretofore filed by the parties have been paid, and that no interest or penalty is due with respect thereto, and that no tax deficiency proceeding is pending or threatened thereon. In the event that any claim is made or liability imposed on account of additional tax, interest or penalty or adjustment arising out of any joint return heretofore filed, which liability is attributable to understated income and/or overstated deductions of one of the parties hereto, which was not known to the other, then such claim or liability shall be the responsibility of the party whose understated income or overstated deductions resulted in the claim or liability and that party hereby agrees to indemnify and hold the other party harmless from any loss, expense (including reasonable attorney's fees and disbursements) and damage on account thereof.

2. The parties hereby agree that they will file separate income tax returns for the year 19___ and for any subsequent year during which the parties shall remain married to each other.

3. The parties further agree that they will cooperate with each other in the event that any audit, claim, tax deficiency or other proceeding is brought by the relevant taxing authorities against the parties, or either of them, on account of any joint return heretofore filed. The parties further agree that the costs and expenses of defending such a proceeding shall be equally borne by the parties.

ARTICLE VII
DEBTS

1. The Wife assumes and henceforth will be solely responsible for the following joint debts of both parties: *[Set forth details]*.

2. The Husband assumes and henceforth will be solely responsible for the following joint debts of both parties: *[Set forth details]*

3. Except as otherwise expressly stated herein, the Wife represents, warrants and covenants that she has not heretofore, nor will she hereafter, incur or contract any debt, charge, obligation or liability whatsoever for which the Husband, his legal representatives, or his property or estate is, or may become, liable. The Wife agrees to indemnify and hold the Husband harmless from all loss, expense (including reasonable attorney's fees) and damages in connection with or arising out of a breach by the Wife of her foregoing representation, warranty and covenant.

4. Except as otherwise expressly stated herein, the Husband represents, warrants and covenants that she has not heretofore, nor will she hereafter, incur or contract any debt, charge, obligation or liability whatsoever for which the Wife, his legal representatives, or his property or estate is, or may become, liable. The Husband agrees to indemnify and hold the Wife harmless from all loss, expense (including reasonable attorney's fees) and damages in connection with or arising out of a breach by the Husband of his foregoing representation, warranty and covenant.

ARTICLE VIII
INDEPENDENT REPRESENTATION

The parties hereto acknowledge that the Wife has been represented by the attorney named below, an attorney of the Wife's own choosing, and that said attorney has prepared this Agreement based upon the terms and conditions agreed to by the parties as the result of direct negotiations between them. The Husband hereby acknowledges that he has been afforded ample opportunity to study and review the provisions of this Agreement and, in connection with his review of this Agreement, has consulted with the attorney named below, an attorney of his own choosing, and has had said attorney advise him with respect thereto. Further, the parties acknowledge that certain revisions and changes have been made as a result of discussions between the attorneys and the parties. Each party shall be solely responsible for the payment of his or her own attorney's fees for services rendered in connection with the negotiation, preparation, and review of this Agreement and the matrimonial issues and disputes that have previously arisen between the parties. Each party shall be solely responsible for the payment of his or her own attorney's fees for services rendered in connection with any matrimonial action which may hereafter be brought by one of the parties hereto against the other party hereto. Each of the parties hereby warrants and represents to the other that he or she has dealt with no other attorney(s) for whose services the other is or may become liable and agrees to indemnify and hold the other harmless of all loss, expenses (including reasonable attorney's fees and disbursements) and damages in the event of a breach by a party of such representation and warranty. However, notwithstanding anything in this Article to the contrary, in the event that either party shall default in any of his or her obligations under this Agreement, or if he or she shall challenge unsuccessfully the validity of this Agreement or its interpretation, then that party shall be liable for the cost and expenses of the other party as a result thereof, including but not limited to, reasonable attorney's fees and disbursements. The name, address and telephone numbers for the attorneys representing each party are as follows:

(a) Attorney for Husband:

(b) Attorney for Wife:

ARTICLE IX
MUTUAL RELEASES

1. Except as otherwise expressly provided herein, each party hereby releases, remixes, and forever discharges the other of and from any and all causes of action, claims, rights, or demands, whatsoever, in law or in equity, which either of the parties hereto ever had, or now has, against the other, except (a) nothing herein contained shall be deemed to prevent either party from enforcing the terms of this Agreement or from asserting such claims as are reserved by this Agreement to each party

against the other or the estate of the other; provided, however, that the claims so asserted arise out of a breach of this Agreement; and (b) nothing herein contained shall impair or waive or release any and all causes of action for a divorce, annulment, or separation or any defenses which either may have to any divorce, annulment or separation action which may be hereafter brought by the other.

2. The Husband shall have the right to dispose of his property by Last Will and Testament in such manner as he may, in his uncontrolled discretion deem proper, and with the same force and effect as if the Wife had died during his lifetime. The Husband covenants that he will permit any Will of the Wife to be probated, and if she shall die intestate, will allow administration of her personal estate and effects to be taken out by the person or persons who would have been entitled thereto had he died during her lifetime.

3. The Wife shall have the right to dispose of her property by Last Will and Testament in such manner as she may, in her uncontrolled discretion deem proper, and with the same force and effect as if the Husband had died during her lifetime. The Wife covenants that she will permit any Will of the Husband to be probated, and if he shall die intestate, will allow administration of his personal estate and effects to be taken out by the person or persons who would have been entitled thereto had he died during her lifetime.

ARTICLE X
RELEASE AND WAIVER OF MARITAL PROPERTY

Each party does hereby waive and release any statutory right or interest he or she may have by force of law, or otherwise, as a surviving spouse, in the property, real or personal, of which the other party shall die seized or possessed, or to which either of them or their estates may in any way be entitled an each party further waives the right that he or she may now or may hereafter have pursuant to (the applicable state's estate law), or any comparable provisions of the laws of any other state which may have jurisdiction over the estate of either party hereto on his or her death, as such sections or provisions now exist or may hereafter be amended, to elect to take in contravention of the terms of any Last Will and Testament of the other party, including any Last Will and Testament now executed or which may hereafter be executed.

ARTICLE XI
RECONCILIATION

1. This Agreement shall not be invalidated or otherwise affected by reconciliation between the parties hereto, or resumption of marital relations between them, unless said reconciliation or said resumption be documented in a written statement executed and acknowledged by the parties with respect to said reconciliation and/or resumption and, in addition, setting forth that they are canceling this Agreement. This Agreement shall not be invalidated or otherwise affected by an decree or judgment of separation or divorce made in any court in any action presently pending or which may hereafter be instituted by either party against the other for separation or divorce.

2. Each party agrees that the provisions of this Agreement shall be submitted to any Court in which either may be seeking or may seek a judgment or decree of divorce, annulment, separation or a judgment that otherwise affects their marital status. Each party agrees further that, in the event that a judgment or decree of divorce, annulment, separation, or a judgment or decree which otherwise affects their marital status, is entered, the provisions of this Agreement shall be incorporated into said judgment or decree with such specificity as the Court may deem permissible and by reference as may be appropriate under the law and rules of the Court. However, notwithstanding such incorporation, the obligations and covenants of this Agreement shall survive any decree or judgment of divorce, annulment, or separation or any decree or judgment which otherwise affects their marital status and shall not merge therein, and this Agreement may be enforced independently of said decree or judgment in accordance with the terms hereof.

ARTICLE XII
GENERAL PROVISIONS

1. This Agreement shall be binding upon the parties, the heirs, personal representatives and assigns.

2. This Agreement shall be construed according to the laws of the State of *[Name of applicable State]*, as an agreement made and to be executed within such State.

3. Each party shall take any and all steps and execute and deliver any and all instruments and documents which may be reasonably required for the purpose of giving full force and effect to the provisions of this Agreement.

4. Each party has made independent inquiry into the complete financial circumstances of the other and is fully informed of the income, assets, property and financial prospects of the other.

5. This Agreement constitutes the entire understanding of the parties and no modification or waiver of its terms shall be valid unless in writing and signed by the parties. This Agreement shall not be subject to modification by any court of law. No waiver of a breach or default of any provision of this Agreement shall be deemed a waiver of any subsequent breach or default.

6. In the event that any provision of this Agreement is held to be illegal, invalid, unenforceable, or against public policy, the remaining provisions of the Agreement shall remain valid and enforceable.

7. Social Security Numbers:

(a) Husband:

(b) Wife:

8. This Agreement contains the entire understanding of the parties, and there are no representations, warranties, covenants or undertakings other than those expressly set forth herein.

9. This Agreement may be executed simultaneously in counterparts, each of which shall be deemed to be an original.

IN WITNESS WHEREOF, the parties hereto have set their hands and seals the day and year first written above.

BY: _____
[SIGNATURE LINE—HUSBAND]

BY: _____
[SIGNATURE LINE—WIFE]

STATE OF   )

               ss.:

COUNTY OF   )

On the _____ day of _____, 20___, before me personally came [Name of Husband], to me known to be the individual described in and who executed the foregoing instrument, and acknowledged that he executed the same.

_____
[NOTARY PUBLIC]

STATE OF   )

              ss.:

COUNTY OF   )

On the _____ day of _____, 20___ before me personally came *[Name of Wife]*, to me known to be the individual described in and who executed the foregoing instrument, and acknowledged that she executed the same.

_____
   [NOTARY PUBLIC]

FORM 8-4

SAMPLE JOINT CUSTODY AGREEMENT

THIS AGREEMENT, made this___day of_____, 2001, by and between JOHN SMITH, residing at 123 Main Street, White Plains, New York (hereinafter referred to as "Father") and MARY SMITH, residing at 456 Elm Street, White Plains, New York (hereinafter referred to as "Mother"),

WITNESSETH:

WHEREAS, the parties were divorced on the 31st day of December, 2000, in the City of White Plains, County of Westchester, in the State of New York; and

WHEREAS, there is one child born of the marriage, to wit: JOSEPH SMITH, age 8, born on September 19, 1993 (hereinafter referred to as "the child"); and

WHEREAS, the parties desire to resolve the custody arrangements of their minor child;

NOW THEREFORE, in consideration of the promises and undertakings herein set forth both parties do hereby covenant and agree as follows:

1. Father and Mother shall have joint legal custody of their minor child and equal input into all matters relating to the child's health, education and welfare.

2. Father is hereby designated as primary residential custodian of the child.

3. Father shall not relocate the child from the State of New York. If Father desires to relocate outside of the State of New York, Mother shall become the primary residential custodian of the child.

4. Father and Mother agree to share physical custody of the child according to the following schedule:

(a) Every Wednesday throughout the year, except as may conflict with the holiday schedule as set forth in (c) below, the child shall be in the physical custody of the Mother, who will pick up the child at 5:30 p.m., and return the child the following morning at

8:00 a.m., for his timely delivery by Mother to school, or on non-school days, to the custodial residence.

(b) Every other weekend throughout the year, except as may conflict with the holiday schedule as set forth in (c) below, the child shall be in the physical custody of the Mother, who will pick up the child at 5:30 p.m. on Friday, and return the child at 8:00 a.m. on Monday morning, for his timely delivery by Mother to school, or on non-school days, to the custodial residence.

(c) The following holiday schedule shall take precedence over the above regular schedule:

(i) On holidays which fall on a Monday, the child shall remain with the parent who has had the child for that weekend. If the child is in the physical custody of Mother, Mother shall return the child at 8:00 a.m. on Tuesday morning, for his timely delivery by Mother to school, or on non-school days, to the custodial residence.

(ii) Effective as of the date of this Agreement, the child shall spend alternating Thanksgiving Holidays with the Mother in odd-numbered years and the Father in even-numbered years.

(iii) Effective as of the date of this Agreement, the child shall spend alternating Easter Holidays with the Mother in even-numbered years and the Father in odd-numbered years.

(iv) Effective as of the date of this Agreement, the child shall spend alternating Christmas Eve Holidays with the Mother in odd-numbered years and the Father in even-numbered years, beginning at 3:00 p.m. on December 24th through 10:00 a.m. on December 25th.

(v) Effective as of the date of this Agreement, the child shall spend alternating Christmas Day Holidays with the Mother in even-numbered years and the Father in odd-numbered years, beginning at 10:00 a.m. on December 25th through December 26th at 10:00 a.m.

(d) The parties agree to the following vacation schedule:

(i) Each party is entitled to physical custody of the child for one-half of the summer vacation, with the dates to be established no later than May 31st.

(ii) Each party is entitled to physical custody of the child for one-half of the designated spring recess, with the dates and times to be agreed to between the parties.

(iii) Each party is entitled to physical custody of the child for one-half of the designated winter recess, with the dates and times to be agreed to between the parties.

5. The parties may, upon mutual agreement, amend the above schedule to accommodate the demands of work, illness, school schedules, or for other good cause.

IN WITNESS WHEREOF, the parties have signed, sealed and acknowledged this Agreement as of the date first written above.

_____
JOHN SMITH

_____
MARY SMITH

STATE OF NEW YORK   )

COUNTY OF WESTCHESTER   )

On the   day of   , 2001, before me personally came JOHN SMITH and MARY SMITH, to me known and known to me to be the individuals described in and who executed the foregoing instrument, and who acknowledged to me that they executed the same.

_____
NOTARY PUBLIC

FORM 8-5

SAMPLE CUSTODY AGREEMENT CLAUSE CONCERNING RELIGIOUS UPBRINGING

The parties agree that, in order to maintain the continuity of the child's religious affiliation and education, the child will be brought up in the Catholic faith and will continue to attend St. Joan of Arc Elementary School, or in the event that the child shall relocate out of the parish of said school, the child will attend the Catholic parochial school of the parish which serves the child's new home.

FORM 8-6

STATEMENT OF NET WORTH—DIVORCE PROCEEDING

Revised 11/98

         COURT
COUNTY OF   Index No.

_____

                   Plaintiff,   STATEMENT OF
      - against -   NET WORTH
                                   (DRL §236)
                Defendant.
_____ Date of commencement of action
_____

Complete all items, marking "NONE," "INAPPLICABLE" and "UNKNOWN," if appropriate)

STATE OF   COUNTY OF   SS.:

         , the (Petitioner) (Respondent) (Plaintiff) (Defendant) herein, being
duly sworn, deposes and says that the following is an accurate statement as of
_____, of my net worth (assets of whatsoever kind and nature and wherever
situated minus liabilities), statement of income from all sources and statement of
assets transferred of whatsoever kind and nature and wherever situated:

I.   FAMILY DATA:
     (a)   Husband's age _____
     (b)   Wife's age _____
     (c)   Date married _____
     (d)   Date (separated) (divorced) _____
     (e)   Number of dependent children under 21 years _____
     (f)   Names and ages of children
               _____
               _____
               _____
               _____
     (g)   Custody of Children _____Husband _____Wife
     (h)   Minor children of prior marriage: _____Husband _____Wife
     (i)   (Husband) (Wife) (paying) (receiving) $_____ as alimony (maintenance)
          and/or $_____ child support in connection with prior marriage
     (j)   Custody of children of prior marriage:
          Name_____
          Address_____
     (k)   Is marital residence occupied by Husband_____ Wife_____ Both_____
     (l)   Husband's present address
          _____
          Wife's present address
          _____
     (m)   Occupation of Husband _____ Occupation of Wife _____
     (n)   Husband's employer
          _____
     (o)   Wife's employer
          _____
     (p)   Education, training and skills [Include dates of attainment of degrees,
          etc.]
             Husband _____
             Wife _____
     (q)   Husband's health _____
     (r)   Wife's health _____
     (s)   Children's health _____

II.   EXPENSES: (You may elect to list all expenses on a weekly basis or all expenses on a monthly basis, however, you must be consistent. If any items are paid on a monthly basis, divide by 4.3 to obtain weekly payments; if any items are paid on a weekly basis, multiply by 4.3 to obtain monthly payment. Attach additional sheet, if needed. Items included under "Other" should be listed separately with separate dollar amounts.)

Expenses listed [] weekly   [] monthly

(a) Housing
   1. Rent   _____
   2. Mortgage and
      amortization _____
   3. Real estate taxes _____

4. Condominium charges _____
5. Cooperative apartment
   maintenance _____

     Total: Housing

$_____

(b) Utilities
   1. Fuel oil _____
   2. Gas _____
   3. Electricity _____

4. Telephone _____
5. Water _____

     Total: Utilities

$_____

(c) Food
   1. Groceries _____
   2. School lunches _____
   3. Lunches at work _____
   4. Dining Out _____

5. Liquor/alcohol _____
6. Home entertainment _____
7. Other _____ _____

     Total: Food

$_____

(d) Clothing
   1. Husband _____
   2. Wife _____

3. Children _____
4. Other _____
     Total: Clothing

$_____

(e) Laundry
   1. Laundry at home _____
   2. Dry cleaning _____

3. Other _____ _____

     Total: Laundry

$_____

(f) Insurance
   1. Life _____
   2. Homeowner's/tenant's_____
   3. Fire, theft and
      liability _____
   4. Automotive _____
   5. Umbrella policy _____

6. Medical plan _____
7. Dental plan _____
8. Optical plan _____
9. Disability _____
10. Worker's Compensation _____
11. Other _____ _____
     Total: Insurance

$_____

(g) Unreimbursed medical
   1. Medical _____
   2. Dental _____
   3. Optical _____
   4. Pharmaceutical _____

5. Surgical, nursing,
   hospital _____
6. Other _____ _____

     Total: Unreimbursed medical

$_____

(h) Household maintenance
   1. Repairs _____
   2. Furniture, furnishings
      housewares _____
   3. Cleaning supplies _____
   4. Appliances, including
      maintenance _____

5. Painting _____
6. Sanitation/carting _____
7. Gardening/landscaping _____
8. Snow removal _____
9. Extermination _____
10. Other _____ _____

3.

                                        Total: Household maintenance
$_____

  (i) Household help
    1. Babysitter   _____   3. Other _____   _____
    2. Domestic (housekeeper, maid, etc.) _____
                                        Total: Household help
$_____

  (j) Automotive
    Year:_____ Make:_____   Personal: ___ Business: ___
    Year:_____ Make:_____   Personal: ___ Business: ___
    Year:_____ Make:_____   Personal: ___ Business: ___
    1. Payments   _____   4. Car wash   _____
    2. Gas and oil   _____   5. Registration and license_____
    3. Repairs   _____   6. Parking and tolls   _____
              7. Other _____
                                        Total: Automotive
  $_____

  (k) Educational
    1. Nursery and pre-school _____   6. School transportation   _____
    2. Primary and secondary _____   7. School supplies/books   _____
    3. College   _____   8. Tutoring   _____
    4. Post-graduate   _____   9. School events   _____
    5. Religious instruction _____   10. Other _____   _____
                                        Total: Educational
$_____

  (l) Recreational
    1. Summer camp   _____   9. Country club/pool club _____
    2. Vacations   _____   10. Health club   _____
    3. Movies   _____   11. Sporting goods   _____
    4. Theatre, ballet, etc. _____   12. Hobbies   _____
    5. Video rentals   _____   13. Music/dance lessons   _____
    6. Tapes, CD's, etc. _____   14. Sports lessons
    7. Cable television _____   15. Birthday parties   _____
    8. Team sports   _____   16. Other _____   _____
                                        Total: Recreational
$_____

  (m) Income taxes
    1. Federal   _____   3. City   _____
    2. State   _____   4. Social Security and   _____
                                            Medicare
                                        Total: Income taxes
$_____

  (n) Miscellaneous
    1. Beauty parlor/barber _____   9. Union and organi-
    2. Beauty aids/cosmetics,   zation dues

       drug items   _____   10. Commutation and
                                            transportation   _____
    3. Cigarettes/tobacco _____   11. Veterinarian/pet expenses_____
    4. Books, magazines,   12. Child support payments
       newspapers   _____   (prior marriage)   _____
    5. Children's allowances _____   13. Alimony and maintenance payments
    6. Gifts   _____   (prior marriage)   _____
    7. Charitable contributions_____   14. Loan payments   _____
    8. Religious organization   15. Unreimbursed business
       dues   _____   expenses   _____
                                        Total: Miscellaneous
$_____

4.

(o) Other
     1. _____   3. _____   _____
     2. _____   4. _____   _____
                              Total: Other   _____
$_____

                              TOTAL EXPENSES: $_____
III.   GROSS INCOME: (State source of income and annual amount. Attach addi-
        tional sheet, if needed).

(a) Salary or wages: (State whether income has changed during the year
     preceding date of this affidavit _____. If so, set forth name and address
     of all employers during preceding year and average weekly wage paid by
     each. Indicate overtime earnings separately. Attach previous year's W-2
     or income tax return.)
     _____   _____
     _____   _____

(b) Weekly deductions:
     1. Federal tax .... _____
     2. New York State tax........................ _____
     3. Local tax................................. _____
     4. Social Security........................... _____
     5. Medicare.................................. _____
     6. Other payroll deductions (specify)........ _____
(c) Social Security number _____
(d) Number and names of dependents claimed: _____
(e) Bonus, commissions, fringe benefits (use of auto,
     memberships, etc.).......................... _____
(f) Partnership, royalties, sale of assets
     (income and installment payments).......... _____
(g) Dividends and interest (state whether taxable
     or not).................................... _____
(h) Real estate (income only)................... _____
(i) Trust, profit sharing and annuities
     (principal distribution and income)........ _____
(j) Pension (income only)...................... _____
(k) Awards, prizes, grants (state whether taxable) _____
(l) Bequests, legacies and gifts................ _____
(m) Income from all other sources............... _____
     (including alimony, maintenance or child support
     from prior marriage)
(n) Tax preference items:
     1. Long term capital gain deduction.......... _____
     2. Depreciation, amortization or depletion.... _____
     3. Stock options -- excess of fair market
        value over amount paid................... _____
(o) If any child or other member of your household
     is employed, set forth name and that person's
     annual income
(p) Social Security............................. _____
(q) Disability benefits......................... _____
(r) Public assistance........................... _____
(s) Other....................................... _____

                              TOTAL INCOME:

_____
IV.   ASSETS: (If any asset is held jointly with spouse or another, so state,
        and set forth your respective shares. Attach additional sheets, if

5.

needed.)

A. Cash Accounts
    Cash
      1.1   a.
Location_____
          b. Source of funds_____
          c. Amount_____
                                   $_____
                             Total: Cash
   $_____

    Checking Accounts
      2.1 a. Financial institution _____
          b. Account number _____
          c. Title holder _____
          d. Date opened_____
          e. Source of Funds_____
          f. Balance_____
                            $_____

      2.2   a. Financial institution
_____
          b. Account number _____
          c. Title Holder _____
          d. Date opened_____
          e. Source of Funds_____
          f. Balance_____
                       $_____
                  Total: Checking $_____

    Savings accounts (including individual, joint, totten trust,
certificates of deposit, treasury notes)
      3.1 a. Financial institution _____
          b. Account number _____
          c. Title holder _____
          d. Type of account_____
          e. Date opened_____
          f. Source of funds_____
          g. Balance_____
                       $_____

      3.2 a. Financial institution _____
          b. Account number _____
          c. Title holder _____
          d. Type of account_____
          e. Date opened_____
          f. Source of funds_____
          g. Balance_____
                     $_____
                  Total: Savings
$_____

    Security deposits, earnest money, etc.
      4.1 a. Location _____
          b. Title owner _____
          c. Type of deposit _____
          e. Source of funds_____
          f. Date of deposit _____
          g. Amount_____
                    $_____
                  Total: Security
$_____   Deposits, etc.
    Other
      5.1 a. Location _____

6.

```
        b. Title owner _____
        c. Type of account _____
        d. Source of funds_____
        e. Date of deposit _____
        f. Amount_____
                                    $_____
                        Total:  Other
$_____


                        Total:  Cash Accounts
$_____
B.  Securities
        Bonds, notes, mortgages
           1.1 a. Description of security _____
               b. Title holder _____
               c. Location _____
               d. Date of acquisition _____
               e. Original price or value _____
               f. Source of funds to acquire _____
               g. Current value_____
                                    $_____
                        Total: Bonds, notes, etc.
$_____


        Stocks, options and commodity contracts
           2.1 a. Description of security _____
               b. Title holder _____
               c. Location _____
               d. Date of acquisition _____
               e. Original price or value _____
               f. Source of funds to acquire _____
               g. Current value_____
                                    $_____

           2.2 a. Description of security _____
               b. Title holder _____
               c. Location _____
               d. Date of acquisition _____
               e. Original price or value _____
               f. Source of funds to acquire _____ .
               g. Current value_____
                                    $_____

           2.3 a. Description of security _____
                               b. Title holder _____
               c. Location _____
               d. Date of acquisition _____
               e. Original price or value _____
               f. Source of funds to acquire _____
               g. Current value_____
                                    $_____
                        Total: Stocks, options, etc.
$_____

        Broker margin accounts
           3.1 a. Name and address of broker_____
               b. Title holder_____
               c. Date account opened _____
               d. Original value of account _____
               e. Source of funds _____
               f. Current value_____
                                    $_____
                        Total: Margin accounts
```

7.

$_____

Total value of securities:

$_____

C. Loans to others and accounts receivable
    1.1 a. Debtor's name and address _____
        b. Original amount of loan or debt _____
        c. Source of funds from which loan made or origin
          of debt _____
        d. Date payment(s) due_____
        e. Current amount due_____ $_____

    1.2 a. Debtor's name and address_____
        b. Original amount of loan or debt _____
        c. Source of funds from which loan made or origin
          of debt _____
        d. Date payment(s) due_____
        e. Current amount due_____ $_____
                Total: Loans and accounts receivable $_____

D. Value of interest in any business
    1.1 a. Name and address of business _____
        b. Type of business (corporate, partnership, sole
          proprietorship or other)_____
        c. Your capital contribution _____
        d. Your percentage of interest _____
        e. Date of acquisition _____
        f. Original price or value _____
        g. Source of funds to acquire _____
        h. Method of valuation _____
        i. Other relevant information_____
        j. Current net worth of business _____ $_____
                Total: Value of business interest $_____

E. Cash surrender value of life insurance
    1.1 a. Insurer's name and address _____
        b. Name of insured _____
        c. Policy number _____
        d. Face amount of policy _____
        e. Policy owner _____
        f. Date of acquisition _____
        g. Source of funding to acquire_____
        h. Current cash surrender value _____ $_____
                Total: Value of life insurance

$_____

F. Vehicles (automobile, boat, plane, truck, camper, etc.)
    1.1 a. Description _____
        b. Title owner _____
        c. Date of acquisition _____
        d. Original price _____
        e. Source of funds to acquire_____
        f. Amount of current lien unpaid _____
        g. Current fair market value _____ $_____

    1.2 a. Description _____
        b. Title owner _____
        c. Date of acquisition _____

8.

```
         d. Original price _____
         e. Source of funds to acquire _____
         f. Amount of current lien unpaid _____
         g. Current fair market value _____  $_____
                           Total:  Value of Vehicles           $_____
   G. Real estate (including real property, leaseholds, life estates, etc. at market
      value -- do not deduct any mortgage)
         1.1 a. Description _____
             b. Title owner _____
             c. Date of acquisition _____
             d. Original price _____
             e. Source of funds to acquire _____
             f. Amount of mortgage or lien unpaid _____

             g. Estimated current market value _____  $_____

         1.2 a. Description _____
             b. Title owner _____
             c. Date of acquisition _____
             d. Original price _____
             e. Source of funds to acquire _____
             f. Amount of mortgage or lien unpaid _____

             g. Estimated current market value _____  $_____

         1.3 a. Description _____
             b. Title owner _____
             c. Date of acquisition _____
             d. Original price _____
             e. Source of funds to acquire _____
             f. Amount of mortgage or lien unpaid _____

             g. Estimated current market value _____  $_____
                           Total:  Value of real estate
$_____

   H. Vested interests in trusts (pension, profit sharing, legacies, deferred
compensation
      and others)
         1.1 a. Description of trust _____
             b. Location of assets _____
             c. Title owner _____
             d. Date of acquisition _____
             e. Original investment _____
             f. Source of funds _____
             g. Amount of unpaid liens _____
             h. Current value _____  $_____

         1.2 a. Description of trust _____
             b. Location of assets _____
             c. Title owner _____
             d. Date of acquisition _____
             e. Original investment _____
             f. Source of funds _____
             g. Amount of unpaid liens _____
             h. Current value _____  $_____
                           Total:  Vested interest in trusts
$_____
```

9.

I. Contingent interests (stock options, interests subject to life estates, prospective
      inheritances, etc.)
         1.1 a. Description _____
            b. Location _____
            c. Date of vesting _____
            d. Title owner _____
            e. Date of acquisition _____
            f. Original price or value _____
            g. Source of funds to acquire _____
            h. Method of valuation _____
            i. Current value _____ $_____
                          Total: Contingent interests
$_____

J. Household furnishings
         1.1 a. Description _____
            b. Location _____
            c. Title owner _____
            d. Original price _____
            e. Source of funds to acquire _____
            f. Amount of lien unpaid _____
            g. Current value _____ $_____
                          Total: Household furnishings $_____

K. Jewelry, art, antiques, precious objects, gold and precious metals (only if valued
      at more than $500)
         1.1 a. Description _____
            b. Title owner _____
            c. Location _____
            d. Original price or value _____
            e. Source of funds to acquire _____
            f. Amount of lien unpaid _____
            g. Current value _____ $_____

         1.2 a. Description _____
            b. Title owner _____
            c. Location _____
            d. Original price or value _____
            e. Source of funds to acquire _____
            f. Amount of lien unpaid _____
            g. Current value _____ $_____
                        Total: Jewelry, art, etc.: $_____

L. Other (e.g., tax shelter investments, collections, judgments, causes of action,
    patents, trademarks, copyrights, and any other asset not hereinabove itemized)
         1.1 a. Description _____
            b. Title owner _____
            c. Location _____
            d. Original price or value _____
            e. Source of funds to acquire _____
            f. Amount of lien unpaid _____
            g. Current value _____ $_____

         1.2 a. Description _____
            b. Title owner _____
            c. Location _____
            d. Original price or value _____

10.

    e. Source of funds to acquire _____
    f. Amount of lien unpaid _____
    g. Current value _____ $_____

$_____
                                Total: Other

                           TOTAL: ASSETS $_____

V. LIABILITIES

A. Accounts payable
    1.1 a.   Name and address of
creditor_____
        b. Debtor_____
        c. Amount of original debt _____
        d. Date of incurring debt _____
        e. Purpose _____
        f. Monthly or other periodic payment _____
        g. Amount of current debt_____ $_____

    1.2 a.   Name and address of
creditor_____
        b. Debtor_____
        c. Amount of original debt _____
        d. Date of incurring debt _____
        e. Purpose _____
        f. Monthly or other periodic payment _____
        g. Amount of current debt_____ $_____

    1.3 a.   Name and address of
creditor_____
        b. Debtor_____
        c. Amount of original debt _____
        d. Date of incurring debt _____
        e. Purpose _____
        f. Monthly or other periodic payment _____
        g. Amount of current debt_____ $_____

    1.4 a.   Name and address of
creditor_____
        b. Debtor_____
        c. Amount of original debt _____
        d. Date of incurring debt _____
        e. Purpose _____
        f. Monthly or other periodic payment _____
        g. Amount of current debt_____ $_____

    1.5 a.   Name and address of
creditor_____
        b. Debtor_____
        c. Amount of original debt _____
        d. Date of incurring debt _____
        e. Purpose _____
        f. Monthly or other periodic payment _____
        g. Amount of current debt_____ $_____

                        Total: Accounts payable
$_____

11.

B. Notes payable
    1.1 a. Name and address of note holder_____
        b. Debtor_____
        c. Amount of original debt _____
        d. Date of incurring debt _____
        e. Purpose _____
        f. Monthly or other periodic payment_____
        g. Amount of current debt_____ $_____

    1.2 a. Name and address of note holder_____
        b. Debtor_____
        c. Amount of original debt _____
        d. Date of incurring debt _____
        e. Purpose _____
        f. Monthly or other periodic payment _____
        g. Amount of current debt_____ $_____
                           Total: Notes payable

$_____

C. Installment accounts payable (security agreements, chattel mortgages)
    1.1 a. Name and address of creditor _____
        b. Debtor_____
        c. Amount of original debt _____
        d. Date of incurring debt _____
        e. Purpose _____
        f. Monthly or other periodic payment_____
        g. Amount of current debt_____ $_____

    1.2 a. Name and address of creditor _____
        b. Debtor_____
        c. Amount of original debt _____
        d. Date of incurring debt _____
        e. Purpose _____
         f. Monthly or other periodic payment _____
        g. Amount of current debt_____ $_____
                      Total: Installment accounts

$_____

D. Brokers' margin accounts
    1.1 a. Name and address of broker _____
        b. Amount of original debt _____
        c. Date of incurring debt _____
        d. Purpose _____
        e. Monthly or other periodic payment_____
        f. Amount of current debt_____ $_____
                      Total: Brokers' margin accounts

$_____

E. Mortgages payable on real estate
    1.1 a. Name and address of mortgagee _____
        b. Address of property mortgaged _____
        c. Mortgagor(s) _____
        d. Original debt _____
        e. Date of incurring debt _____
        f. Monthly or other periodic payment _____
        g. Maturity Date _____
        h. Amount of current debt_____ $_____
    1.2 a. Name and address of mortgagee _____
        b. Address of property mortgaged _____

12.

```
        c. Mortgagor(s) _____
        d. Original debt _____
        e. Date of incurring debt _____
        f. Monthly or other periodic payment _____
        g. Maturity date _____
        h. Amount of current debt_____ $_____
                                     Total:  Mortgages payable
$_____

F.  Taxes payable
      1.1 a. Description of tax _____
          b. Amount of tax _____
          c. Date due _____
                                     Total: Taxes payable
$_____

G.  Loans on life insurance policies
      1.1 a. Name and address of insurer _____
          b. Amount of loan _____
          c. Date incurred _____
          d. Purpose _____
          e. Name of borrower _____
          f. Monthly or other periodic payment ____
          g. Amount of current debt _____ $_____
                                     Total:  Life insurance loans
$_____

H.  Other liabilities
      1.1 a. Description _____
          b. Name and address of creditor _____
          c. Debtor _____
          d. Original amount of debt _____
          e. Date incurred _____
          f. Purpose _____
          g. Monthly or other periodic payment ____
          h. Amount of current debt _____ $_____

      1.2 a. Description _____
          b. Name and address of creditor _____
          c. Debtor _____
          d. Original amount of debt _____
          e. Date incurred _____
          f. Purpose _____
          g. Monthly or other periodic payment ____
          h. Amount of current debt _____ $_____
                                     Total:  Other liabilities
$_____


                            TOTAL LIABILITIES:     $_____
```

NET WORTH

```
    TOTAL ASSETS:                           $_____

    TOTAL LIABILITIES:        (minus)    ($_____)

    NET WORTH:                              $_____
```

13.

VI.   ASSETS TRANSFERRED: (List all assets transferred in any manner during the preceding three years, or length of the marriage, whichever is shorter [transfers in the routine course of business which resulted in an exchange of assets of substantially equivalent value need not be specifically disclosed where such assets are otherwise identified in the statement of net worth]).

Description of Property	To Whom Transferred and Relationship to Transferee	Date of Transfer	Value
_____	_____	_____	
_____	_____	_____	
_____	_____	_____	
_____	_____	_____	
_____			

VII.   SUPPORT REQUIREMENTS:

(a)   Deponent is at present (paying)(receiving) $_____ per (week)(month), and prior to separation (paid)(received) $_____ per (week)(month) to cover expenses for

_____

_____

These payments are being made (voluntarily)(pursuant to court order or judgment)(pursuant to separation agreement), and there are (no) arrears outstanding (in the sum of $_____ to date).

(b)   Deponent requests for support of each child $_____ per (week)(month). Total for children $_____.

(c)   Deponent requests for support of self $_____ per (week)(month).
(d)   The day of the (week)(month) on which payment should be made is _____.

VIII. COUNSEL FEE REQUIREMENTS:

(a)   Deponent requests for counsel fee and disbursements the sum of _____.
(b)   Deponent has paid counsel the sum of $_____ and has agreed with counsel concerning fees as follows:

_____

_____

(c)   There is (not) a retainer agreement or written agreement relating to payment of legal fees. (A copy of any such agreement must be annexed.)

IX.   ACCOUNTANT AND APPRAISAL FEES REQUIREMENTS:

(a)   Deponent requests for accountants' fees and disbursements the sum of $_____. (Include basis for fee, e.g., hourly rate, flat rate)
(b)   Deponent requests for appraisal fees and disbursements the sum of $_____. (Include basis for fee, e.g., hourly rate, flat rate)
(c)   Deponent requires the services of an accountant for the following reasons:

_____

(d)   Deponent requires the services of an appraiser for the following reasons:

_____

14.

X.   Other data concerning the financial circumstances of the parties that should be brought to the attention of the Court are:

_____

_____

_____

_____

_____

The foregoing statements and a rider consisting of _____ page(s) annexed hereto and made part hereof, have been carefully read by the undersigned who states that they are true and correct.

_____

(Petitioner)   (Respondent)
(Plaintiff)   (Defendant)

Sworn to before me this
    day of   , 19

_____

_____

SIGNATURE OF ATTORNEY

_____

ATTORNEY'S NAME (PRINT OR TYPE)

_____

_____

ATTORNEY'S ADDRESS & TELEPHONE NUMBER

FORM 8-7

PETITION FOR ADOPTION—PRIVATE PLACEMENT

D.R.L.§§ 111, 111-a, 112, 115
S.C.P.A. § 1725(1)

Form 1-C
(Petition-Private
-Placement)
12/97

SURROGATE'S COURT OF THE STATE OF NEW YORK
COUNTY OF
....

In the Matter of Adoption of
A Child Whose First Name Is

(Docket)(File) No.

PETITION FOR
ADOPTION
(Private-Placement)

....

The Petitioner(s) respectfully allege(s) to this Court that :

[Delete inapplicable provisions.]:

    1. Petitioning adoptive parent [specify name]:

        a. resides at [specify address, including county]:

        b. is of full age, having been born on [specify date of birth]:

        c. is (unmarried)
            (married to [specify name]:   and living together
            (married to [specify name]:   and living
separate and apart pursuant to a decree or judgment of separation or pursuant to a separation
agreement subscribed by the parties thereto and acknowledged or proved in the form required
to entitle a deed to be recorded);
            (married to [specify name]:   and living separate and
apart for at least three years prior to   commencement of the proceeding);

        d. is of the following religious faith, if any:

        e. is engaged in the following occupation [specify]:   and earns $
(of which $ is support and maintenance to be received from the Commissioner of Social
Services on behalf of the adoptive child).

    2. Petitioning adoptive parent [specify name]:

        a. resides at [specify address, including county]:

Form 1-C page 2

    b. is of full age, having been born on [specify date of birth]:

    c. is (unmarried)
        (married to [specify name]:   and living together
        (married to [specify name]:   and living separate
and apart pursuant to a decree or judgment of separation or pursuant to a separation agreement subscribed by the parties thereto and acknowledged or proved in the form required to entitle a deed to be recorded);
        (married to [specify name]:   and living separate and apart for at least three years prior to commencement of the proceeding);

    d. is of the following religious faith, if any:

        e. is engaged in the following occupation [specify]:   and earns $ in approximate annual income (of which $ is support and maintenance to be received from the Commissioner of Social Services on behalf of the adoptive child).

    3. The full name, date and place of birth of the adoptive child is

        [attach certified copy of birth certificate]

    4. Upon information and belief, the religious faith of the adoptive child, if any, is

    5. The following is information, as nearly as can be ascertained, concerning the birth or legal parents of the adoptive child:

        (a) Full name and last known address

Parent (specify full name and address, if known):

Parent (specify full name and address, if known):

        (b) Age and date of birth

Form 1-C page 3

Parent (specify name):
Parent (specify name):

     (c) Heritage (specify nationality, ethnic background,   race)

Parent (specify name):
Parent (specify name):

     (d)   Religious faith, if any

Parent (specify name):
Parent (specify name):

     (e)   Education (specify number of years of school or degrees completed at time of birth of adoptive child)

Parent (specify name):_____
Parent (specify name):_____

     (f)   General physical appearance at time of birth of adoptive child (height, weight, color of hair, eyes, skin)

Parent (specify name):
     Ht:_____ Wt:_____
     Hair Color: _____ Eye Color: _____
     Skin Color: _____

Parent (specify name):
     Ht:_____ Wt: _____
     Hair Color: _____ Eye Color:_____
     Skin Color:_____

     (g) Annex Form 1-D which provides health and medical history at time of birth of adoptive child, including conditions or diseases believed to be hereditary and any drugs or medication taken during pregnancy by child's mother.

     (h) Any other information which may be a factor influencing the adoptive child's present or future well-being, including talents, hobbies and special interests of parents: [attach separate sheet if necessary]

6. The manner in which the adoptive parent(s) obtained the adoptive child is as follows:

7. The adoptive child resided with the adoptive parent(s) from [indicate date]:

8. Other persons living in the household are: [Specify names and dates of birth]:

Form 1-C page 4

9.   The name by which the adoptive child is to be known
is:

10.   Upon information and belief, the adoptive child (has) (has not) been previously
adopted.

11. The full name(s) and address(es) of any person(s) having lawful custody of the
adoptive child, if known (is)(are)

12.   On information and belief, pursuant to Domestic Relations Law §111,

(a) the consent of the birth or legal parent of the adoptive child (is attached hereto) (is not
required because

;)

(b) the consent of the birth or legal parent of the adoptive child (is attached hereto) (is not
required because

;)

(c) the consent(s) of the above-named person(s) having lawful custody of the adoptive child (is
attached hereto) (is not required because

;)

(d) The consent(s) of other person(s)[specify name(s)]:
(is attached hereto) (is not required because
.)

13(a)(The consent of the birth or legal parent [specify name]:   was executed
pursuant to section 115-b(3) of the Domestic Relations Law on
_____, 19_____; the 45th day after execution of the consent is _____,
19_____.

(b) (The consent of the birth or legal parent [specify name]:   was
executed pursuant to Section 115-b(3) of the Domestic Relations Law on
_____, 19_____; the 45th day after execution of the consent is _____,
19_____.)

(14. This court is not the court named in the consent(s) of the parent(s) of the adoptive child,
attached hereto, as the court in which the adoption proceeding will be commenced, but more than
45 days have elapsed since the date of execution of said consent(s) and, on information and
belief, no written notice of revocation has been received by that court.)

(15. That on information and belief said minor child has a (general) (testamentary) guardian.
[state nature, date and place of appointment]:

Form 1-C page 5

16. To the best of the Petitioner(s)' information and belief, there are no persons other than those mentioned herein or in the verified scheduled annexed hereto who are entitled, pursuant to Domestic Relation Law §111(3) and 111-a, to notice of this proceeding (except)

Name: Relationship:
Last known address:

Name   Relationship:
Last known address:

Name   Relationship:
Last known address:

17. Attached hereto and made a part hereof is Form 1-D setting forth all available information comprising the adoptive child's medical history.

18. The placement is subject to the provisions of Social Services Law section(s) (374-a) (382) and the provisions of such section(s) have been complied with. The original approval signed by the Administrator of the Interstate Compact on the Placement of Children is attached hereto.

19. (a) The adoptive parent(s) (has)(have) (no) knowledge that the child or an adoptive parent is the subject of an indicated report or is another person named in an indicated report of child abuse or maltreatment, as such terms are defined in section 412 of the Social Services Law, or has been the subject of or the respondent in a child protective proceeding which resulted in an order finding that the child is an abused or neglected child.

(b) The adoptive parent(s) (has)(have) (no) knowledge of any criminal record concerning themselves or any other adult residing in the household (except)

20. There are no prior or pending proceedings affecting the custody or status of the adoptive child, including any proceedings dismissed or withdrawn, (except) [specify type of proceeding, court, disposition, if any, and date of disposition, if any]:

21. The adoptive child (is)(is not) an Indian child within the meaning of the Indian Child Welfare Act of 1978 (25 U.S.C. §§ 1901-1963).

22. [Insert any additional allegations.]

Form 1-C page 6

WHEREFORE, the Petitioner(s) prays(s) for an order approving granting temporary guardianship of the child to Petitioner(s) and the adoption of the adoptive child [specify first name]:

by the Petitioner(s) and directing that the adoptive child shall be treated in all respects as the child of the Petitioner(s) and directing that the name of the adoptive child be changed and that (s)he shall henceforth be known by the name of
together with such other and further relief as may be just and proper.

Dated: , 19 .

_____/_____
Adoptive Parent: typed or printed name/ signature

_____/_____
Adoptive Parent: typed or printed name / signature

_____/_____
Adoptive child if over 18: typed or printed name / signature

_____/_____
Attorney , if any: typed or printed name/ signature

_____
Attorney's Address and Telephone Number

Form 1-C page 7

VERIFICATION

STATE OF NEW YORK   )
                                          :ss.:
COUNTY OF   )

being duly sworn, says that (he)(she) (they)(is)(are) the Petitioner(s) in the above-named proceeding and that the foregoing petition is true to (his)(her)(their) own knowledge, except as to matters where in stated to be alleged on information and belief and as to those matters (he)(she) (they) believe(s) it to be true.

_____/_____
Adoptive Parent: typed or printed name/ signature

_____/_____
Adoptive Parent: typed or printed name/ signature

_____/_____
Adoptive child if over 18: typed or printed name/ signature

Sworn to before me this
    day of   , 19 .

_____
(Deputy)Clerk of the Court
    Notary Public

Resworn to before me this
    day of   , 19 .

_____
Judge of the   Court

FORM 8-8

CONSENT TO ADOPTION—CHILD OVER AGE 14

D.R.L. § 111(1) (a)

Form 2-D
(Consent of Child -
Private-Placement)
12/97

COURT OF THE STATE OF NEW YORK
COUNTY OF

....

In the Matter of the Adoption of A Child   (Docket)(File) No.
Whose first Name Is

CONSENT OF CHILD
OVER 14
(Private-Placement)

....

The undersigned adoptive child, who is   years old, having been born on
hereby consents to (his) (her) adoption by   ) ,
the petitioning adoptive parent(s) in the above-entitled proceeding.

Dated:

_____
                                                          Child

_____/_____
      Adoptive Parent: typed or printed name/ signature

_____/_____
      Adoptive Parent: typed or printed name / signature

_____/_____
      Adoptive child if over 18: typed or printed name/ signature

_____/_____
      Attorney if any: typed or printed name/signature

_____
      Attorney's Address and Telephone number

Form 2-D page 2

STATE OF NEW YORK   )
                           ss.:
COUNTY OF   )

On this   day of   , 19   , before me personally came
                            , to me known and known to me to be the person described in and who
executed the foregoing instrument and
                        executed the same.   duly acknowledged to me that

_____
          Notary Public

STATE OF NEW YORK   )
                           ss.:
COUNTY OF   )

On this   day of   , 19   , before me personally came
                    proven to me by the oath of   an attorney
admitted to practice in the State of New York to be the person described in and who executed the foregoing
instrument and   duly acknowledged that
executed the same.

_____
     Judge of the   Court

FORM 8-9

ORDER OF ADOPTION

D.R.L. §§111, 112(b), 113, 114   Form 13-B
                                                        (Order of Adoption
                                                        Private-Placement)
                                                        12/97

At a term of the Surrogate's Court of the
State of New York, held in and for the
County of   ,
at   New York
on   , 19   .

PRESENT:
    Hon.
        Judge

In the Matter of the Adoption of   (Docket) (File) No.
A Child Whose First Name Is

                                                        ORDER OF
                                                        ADOPTION
                                                        (Private-Placement)

The Petition of   (and
), verified the   day of   , 19   , having been duly
presented to this Court, together with an agreement on the part of the petitioning adoptive
parent(s) to adopt and treat as (his)(her)(their) own lawful child and whose birth day is
            19   , and who was born at
as set forth in the petition for adoption herein, said petition having been attached thereto
and made a part thereof a document setting forth all available information comprising the
adoptive child's medical history; together with the affidavit(s) of

and the consent(s) of

        AND, although (his)(her)(their) consent(s) (is)(are) not required, the Court
having given notice of the proposed adoption to

                        [recite facts relative thereto]

Form 13-B Page 2

AND the aforesaid petitioning adoptive parents and the adoptive child and all other persons whose consents are required as aforesaid having personally appeared before this Court for examination, except

AND an investigation having been ordered and made and the written report of such investigation having been filed with the Court, as required by the Domestic Relations Law;

(AND the Court having (shortened)(dispensed with) the six-month waiting period between its receiving the petition to adopt and this order of adoption, pursuant to section 116 of the Domestic Relations Law, because

;)

AND the adoptive child having resided with the petitioning adoptive parent(s) since   (and the judge having dispensed with the six-month period of residency with the adoptive parent(s), pursuant to section 112 and 116 of the Domestic Relations Law because

(AND the court having inquired of the statewide central register of child abuse and maltreatment and having been informed that the (child) (adoptive parent(s)) (is)(are)(not) a subject of or another person named in an indicated report filed with such register as such terms are defined in section 412 of the Social Services Law, (AND there being available to this Court findings of a court inquiry made within the preceding twelve months, of the statewide central register of child abuse and maltreatment that the (child) (adoptive parent(s)) (is)(are) (not) a subject of or another parson named in an indicated report filed with such register as such terms are defined in section 412 of the Social Services Law) and the Court having given due consideration to any information contained therein;

Form 13-B Page 3

      AND this Court being satisfied that the best interests of the adoptive child will be promoted by the adoption and that there is no reasonable objection to the proposed change of the name of the adoptive child;

      NOW, on motion of
Attorney for the petitioners) herein, and upon all the papers and proceedings herein, it is

      ORDERED that the petition of   (and
)for the adoption of
a person born on   , 19   , at
                , be and the same hereby is allowed and approved;
and it is further

      ORDERED that the said adoptive child shall henceforth be regarded and treated in all respects as the lawful child of the said adoptive parent(s); and it is further

      ORDERED that the name of the said adoptive child be and the same hereby is changed to   and that
the said adoptive child shall hereafter be known by that name; and it is further

      (ORDERED that the Clerk prepare, certify and deliver to
              a copy of this order; and it is further)

      ORDERED that the child's medical history, heritage of the parents, which shall include nationality, ethnic background and race; education, which shall be the number of years of school completed by the parents at the time of the birth of the adoptive child; general physical appearance of the parents at the time of the birth of the adoptive child, including height, weight, color of hair, eyes, skin; occupation of the parents at the time of birth of the adoptive child; health and medical history of the parents at the time of birth of the adoptive child, including all available information setting forth conditions or diseases believed to be hereditary, any drugs or medication taken during pregnancy by the mother; and other information which may be a factor influencing the child's present or future well-being, talents, hobbies and special interests of the parents as contained in the petition shall be furnished to the adoptive parents; and it is

Form 13-B Page 4

ORDERED that this order, together with all other papers pertaining to the adoption, shall be filed and kept as provided in the Domestic Relations Law and shall not be subject to access or inspections except as provided in said Law.

ENTER

_____
Surrogate

Dated: , 19

FORM 8-10

CERTIFICATE OF ADOPTION

D.R.L. §114

Form 14
(Certificate of Adoption)
12/97

SURROGATE'S COURT OF THE STATE OF NEW YORK
COUNTY OF

CERTIFICATE OF ADOPTION

I,   , Clerk of the
         Court of   County, do hereby certify that I have inspected the records
of this Court and find that:

AN ORDER OF ADOPTION was signed on the   day of   , 19   , by Honorable
                    , Judge of the   Court of the County of   , granting the
petition of   (and   ), adoptive parent(s) of a child now
known and called by the name of   , who was born at   , on
the   day of   , 19   .

This certificate as to the facts recited herein shall have the same force and effect as a
certified copy of an order of adoption.

IN TESTIMONY WHEREOF, I have hereunto set my hand
and affixed the seal of the   Court
of the County of   this
day of   , 19   .

_____
Clerk of the   Court
of the County of

CHAPTER 9
REAL ESTATE AND LANDLORD-TENANT MATTERS

FORM 9-1

AGENCY DISCLOSURE AND ACKNOWLEDGEMENT FORMS REGARDING REAL ESTATE AGENCY RELATIONSHIPS

Before you enter into a discussion with a real estate agent regarding a real estate transaction, you should understand what type of agency relationship you wish to have with that agent. Most states have laws which require real estate licensees who are acting as agents of buyers or sellers of property to advise the potential buyers or sellers with whom they work of the nature of their agency relationship and the rights and obligations it creates.

SELLER'S AGENT

If you are interested in selling real property, you can engage a real estate agent as a seller's agent. A seller's agent, including a listing agent under a listing agreement with the seller, acts solely on behalf of the seller. You can authorize a seller's agent to do other things including the right to hire subagents, broker's agents or work with other agents such as buyer's agents on a cooperative basis. A subagent or "cooperating agent" is one who has agreed to work with the seller's agent, often through a multiple listing service. A subagent may work in a different real estate office.

A seller's agent has, without limitation, the following fiduciary duties to the seller: reasonable care, undivided loyalty, confidentiality, full disclosure, obedience, and a duty to account.

The obligations of an agent are also subject to any specific provision set forth in an agreement between the agent and the seller.

In dealing with the buyer, a seller's agent should:

(a) exercise reasonable skill and care in performance of the agent's duties;

(b) deal honestly, fairly and in good faith; and

(c) disclose all facts known to the agent materially affecting the value or desirability of property, except as otherwise provided by law.

BUYER'S AGENT

If you are interested in buying real property, you can engage a real estate agent as a buyer's agent. A buyer's agent acts solely on behalf of the buyer. You can authorize a buyer's agent to do other things including the right to hire subagents, broker's agents or work with other agents, such as a seller's agents, on a cooperative basis.

A buyer's agent has, without limitation, the following fiduciary duties to the buyer: reasonable care, undivided loyalty confidentiality, full disclosure, obedience and a duty to account.

The obligations of an agent are also subject to any specific provisions set forth in an agreement between the agent and the buyer.

In dealing with the seller, a buyer's agent should:

(a) exercise reasonable care in performance of the agent's duties;

(b) deal honestly, fairly and in good faith;

(c) disclose all facts known to the agent materially affecting the value or the desirability of the property; and

(d) disclose all facts known to the agent materially affecting the value or desirability of the property, except as otherwise provided by law.

DUAL AGENCY

A real estate agent acting directly or through an associated licensee can be the agent of both the seller and the buyer in a transaction, but only with the knowledge and informed consent in writing of both the seller and the buyer.

In such a dual agency situation, the agent will not be able to provide the full range of fiduciary duties to the buyer and seller. The obligation of an agent is also subject to any specific provisions set forth in an agreement between the agent and the buyer and seller.

An agent acting as a dual agent must explain carefully to both the buyer and seller that the agent is acting for the other party as well. The agent should also explain the possible effects of dual representation, including that by consenting to the dual agency relationship, the buyer and seller are giving up their right to undivided loyalty.

NOTE: A BUYER OR SELLER SHOULD CAREFULLY CONSIDER THE POSSIBLE CONSEQUENCES OF A DUAL AGENCY RELATIONSHIP BEFORE AGREEING TO SUCH REPRESENTATION.

GENERAL CONSIDERATIONS

You should carefully read all agreements to ensure that they adequately express your understanding of the transaction. A real estate agent is a person qualified to advise about real estate. If legal, tax or other advice is desired, consult a competent professional in that field.

Throughout the transaction, you may receive more than one disclosure form. The law requires each agent assisting in the transaction to represent you with this disclosure form. You should read its contents each time it is presented to you, considering the relationship between you and the real estate agent in your specific transaction.

ACKNOWLEDGEMENT OF PROSPECTIVE BUYER

(1) I have received, read and understand this disclosure notice.

(2) I understand that a seller's agent, including a listing agent, is the agent of the seller exclusively, unless the seller and buyer otherwise agree.

(3) I understand that subagents, including subagents participating in a multiple listing service, are agents of the seller exclusively.

(4) I understand that I may engage my own agent to be my buyer's broker.

(5) I understand that the agent presenting this form to me, *[NAME OF REAL ESTATE AGENT]* of *[NAME OF REAL ESTATE BROKERAGE OFFICE]* is:

[Check Applicable Relationship):

_____An agent of the seller

_____ My agent as a buyer's agent

DATED: BY:_____
                                    [SIGNATURE LINE—BUYER]

DATED: BY:_____
                                    [SIGNATURE LINE—BUYER]

ACKNOWLEDGEMENT OF PROSPECTIVE SELLER

(1) I have received, read and understand this disclosure notice.

(2) I understand that a seller's agent, including a listing agent, is the agent of the seller exclusively, unless the seller and buyer otherwise agree.

(3) I understand that subagents, including subagents participating in a multiple listing service, are agents of the seller exclusively.

(4) I understand that a buyer's agent is an agent of the buyer exclusively.

(5) I understand that the agent presenting this form to me, *[NAME OF REAL ESTATE AGENT]* of *[NAME OF REAL ESTATE BROKERAGE OFFICE]* is:

[Check Applicable Relationship):

_____ My agent as a seller's agent

_____ An agent of the buyer

DATED: BY:_____
                                [SIGNATURE LINE—SELLER]

DATED: BY:_____
                                [SIGNATURE LINE—SELLER]

ACKNOWLEDGEMENT OF PROSPECTIVE BUYER AND SELLER TO DUAL AGENCY

(1) I have received, read and understand this disclosure notice.

(2) I understand that a dual agent will be working for both the seller and the buyer.

(3) I understand that I may engage my own agent as a seller's agent or a buyer's agent.

(4) I understand that I am giving up my right to the agent's undivided loyalty.

(5) I have carefully considered the possible consequences of a dual agency relationship.

(6) I understand that the agent presenting this form to me, *[NAME OF REAL ESTATE AGENT]* of *[NAME OF REAL ESTATE BROKERAGE OFFICE]* is a dual agent working for both the buyer and seller, acting as such with consent of both buyer and seller and following full disclosure to the buyer and seller.

DATE: BY:_____
                                [SIGNATURE LINE—SELLER]

DATED: BY:_____
                                [SIGNATURE LINE—SELLER]

DATED: BY:_____
                                [SIGNATURE LINE—BUYER]

DATED: BY:_____
       [SIGNATURE LINE—BUYER]

ACKNOWLEDGEMENT OF THE PARTIES TO THE CONTRACT

(1) I have received, read and understand this disclosure notice.

(2) I understand that the agent presenting this form to me, *[NAME OF REAL ESTATE AGENT]* of *[NAME OF REAL ESTATE BROKERAGE OFFICE]* is:

[Check Applicable Relationship):

_____ An agent of the seller

_____ An agent of the buyer

_____ A dual agent working for both the buyer and seller, acting as such with the consent of both buyer and seller and following full disclosure to the buyer and seller.

(3) I also understand that *[NAME OF REAL ESTATE AGENT]* of *[NAME OF REAL ESTATE BROKERAGE OFFICE]* is:

[Check Applicable Relationship):

_____ An agent of the seller

_____ An agent of the buyer

_____ A dual agent working for both the buyer and seller, acting as such with the consent of both buyer and seller and following full disclosure to the buyer and seller.

DATED: BY: _____
       [SIGNATURE LINE—SELLER]

DATED: BY: _____
       [SIGNATURE LINE—SELLER]

DATED: BY: _____
       [SIGNATURE LINE—BUYER]

DATED: BY: _____
       [SIGNATURE LINE—BUYER]

FORM 9-2

BROKER/SALESPERSON INDEPENDENT CONTRACTOR AGREEMENT

AGREEMENT made this ____ day of _____, 20___, by and between *[Name of Salesperson]*, residing at *[Address]* (hereinafter referred to as the "Salesperson") and *[Name of Real Estate Brokerage Firm]* having a principal place of business at *[Address]* (hereinafter referred to as the "Broker").

WITNESSETH:

WHEREAS, Salesperson and Broker are each respectively duly licensed pursuant to *[Insert applicable law, e.g.: Article 12-A of the Real Property Law of the State of New York]*, and

WHEREAS, the parties hereto have freely and voluntarily entered into this Agreement, without duress.

NOW, THEREFORE, in consideration of the mutual promises herein contained, it is hereby agreed as follows:

(1) Salesperson is engaged as an independent contractor associated with the Broker pursuant to *[Insert applicable law, e.g.: Article 12-A of the Real Property Law of the State of New York]*, and shall be treated as such for all purposes, including but not limited to Federal and State income taxation, withholding tax regulations, unemployment insurance, and worker's compensation coverage.

(2) Salesperson shall:

   (a) be paid a commission on Salesperson's gross sales, if any, without deduction for taxes, which commission shall be directly related to sales or other output;

   (b) not be entitled to a draw against commissions;

   (c) not receive any remuneration related to the number of hours worked; and

   (d) not be treated as an employee with respect to such services for Federal and State income tax purposes.

(3) Salesperson shall be permitted to work such hours as Salesperson may elect to work.

(4) Salesperson shall be permitted to work out of Salesperson 's residence or the offices of Broker or any other location in the sole discretion of Salesperson.

(5) Salesperson shall be free to engage in outside employment.

(6) Broker may provide office facilities and supplies for the use of Salesperson. All other expenses, including but not limited to automobile, travel, and entertainment expenses shall be borne by Salesperson.

(7) Broker may offer initial training and hold periodic sales meetings. The attendance by Salesperson at such sessions shall be at the option of Salesperson.

(8) Broker may offer a group insurance plan, and if Salesperson wishes to participate therein, all premiums shall be paid by Salesperson.

(9) Broker m may elect, but shall be under no obligation, to assign leads to Salesperson on a rotating basis. Salesperson shall be responsible for procuring Salesperson's own leads.

(10) Broker and Salesperson shall comply with the requirements of *[Insert applicable law, e.g.: Article 12-A of the Real Property Law of the State of New York]*, and the regulations pertaining thereto. Such compliance shall not affect Salesperson's status as an independent contractor nor shall such compliance be construed as an indication that Salesperson is an employee of Broker for any purpose whatsoever.

(11) This contract and the association created thereby may be terminated by either party hereto at any time upon notice given by one party to the other.

(12) For purposes of this Agreement, the term "Broker" shall include individual real estate brokers, real estate brokerage companies, real estate brokerage corporations and any other entity acting as a principal broker, and the term "Salesperson" shall include real estate sales agents, and real estate brokers, who, as real estate licensees, associate with and place their real estate license with a principal broker.

(13) This Agreement shall be governed and construed in accordance with the laws of the State of *[STATE NAME]*.

(14) No waiver of any of the provisions of this Agreement or any of the rights or remedies of the parties hereto shall be valid unless such waiver is in writing, signed by the party to be charged therewith.

(15) Whenever in this Agreement any notices are required to be given, such notices shall be in writing and shall be sent by registered mail or certified mail, return receipt requested, to the party entitled to receive the same.

This Agreement and all of its terms, covenants and provisions insofar as applicable, shall be binding upon and inure to the benefit of the parties hereto, their respective heirs, executors, administrators, successors and assigns.

IN WITNESS WHEREOF, the individual parties hereto have hereunto set their hands and seals, and any corporate party has caused this instrument to be signed by a corporate officer and caused its corporate seal to be hereunto affixed, all as of the day and year first above written.

BY: _____

      [SIGNATURE LINE—SALESPERSON]

BY: _____

      [SIGNATURE LINE—BROKER]

FORM 9-3

EXCLUSIVE AGENCY AGREEMENT

THIS AGREEMENT is effective as of the ___ day of _____, 20___, and confirms that *[Name of Homeowner]* ("Homeowners) has appointed *[Name of Real Estate Salesperson]* to act as Agent for the sale of property known as *[Address of property being listed for sale]*.

In return for the Agent's agreement to use Agent's best efforts to sell the above property, the Owner agrees to grant the Agent an exclusive agency to sell this property under the following terms and conditions:

PERIOD OF AGREEMENT

(1) This agreement shall be effective from the above date and shall expire at midnight on *[Insert Expiration Date]*.

PRICE AT WHICH PROPERTY WILL BE OFFERED AND AUTHORITY

(2) The property will be offered for sale at a list price of *[DOLLAR AMOUNT ($xxx)]* Dollars, and shall be sold, subject to negotiation, at such price and upon such terms to which Owner may agree. The word Owner refers to each and all parties who have ownership interest in the property and the undersigned represents they are the sole and exclusive owners and are fully authorized to enter into this agreement.

COMMISSION TO BE PAID AGENT

(3) The Agent shall be entitled to and Owner shall pay to Agent one commission of *[Percentage (x%)]* of the selling price. Both the Owner and Agent acknowledge that the above commission rate was not suggested nor influenced by anyone other than the parties to this Agreement. Owner hereby authorizes Agent to make an offer of cooperation to any other licensed real estate broker with whom Agent wishes to cooperate. Any commission due for a sale brought about by a SubAgent (another broker who is authorized by Agent to assist in the sale of Owner's property) or to an authorized Buyer's Agent shall be paid by the Agent from the commission received by the Agent pursuant to this Paragraph.

The commission offered by Agent to Sub-Agents shall be *[Percentage (x%)]* of the gross selling price. The commission offered by Agent to Buyer's Agent shall be *[Percentage (Leo)]* of the gross selling price.

In the event that Owner authorizes Agent to compensate a Buyer's Agent, Owner acknowledges Owner's understanding that such Buyer's Agent is not representing Owner as Sub-Agent and that the Buyer's Agent will be representing Only the interests of the prospective purchaser.

Owner will not be obligated to pay a commission to Agent if Owner sells Owner's property without the efforts of either Agent, any Sub-Agent or a Buyer's Agent whose services have been authorized by Agent.

OWNER'S OBLIGATIONS AFTER THE EXPIRATION OF THIS AGREEMENT

(4) Owner understands and agrees to pay the commission referred to in paragraph 3, if this property is sold or transferred or is the subject of a contract of sale within _ months after the expiration date of this agreement involving a person with whom the Agent or a Cooperating Broker negotiated or to whom the property was offered, quoted or shown by Agent or any Cooperating Broker during the period of this listing agreement. Owner will not, however, be obligated to pay such commission if Owner enters into a valid Exclusive Listing Agreement with another licensed real estate broker after the expiration of this agreement.

WHO MAY NEGOTIATE FOR OWNER

(5) Owner elects to have all offers submitted through:

　　(i) Agent _____

　　(ii) Cooperating Agent _____

SUBMISSION OF LISTING TO MULTIPLE LISTING SERVICE

(6) Both Owner and Agent agree that the Agent immediately is to submit this listing agreement to the designated Multiple Listing Service, Inc. ("MLS") for dissemination to its Participants. No provision of this agreement is intended to nor shall be understood to establish or imply any contractual relationship between the Owner and the MLS, nor has the MLS in any way participated in any of the terms of this agreement, including the commission to be paid. Owner acknowledges that the Agent's ability to submit this listing to the MLS, or to maintain such listing amongst those included in any compilation of listing information published by the MLS, is subject to Agent's continued status as a

member in good standing of the designated Board of Realtors, Inc., and Agent's status as a Participant in good standing of the MLS.

FAIR HOUSING

(7) Agent and Owner agree to comply fully with local, state and federal fair housing laws against discrimination on the basis of race, color, religion, sex, national origin, handicap, age, marital status and/or familial status, children or other prohibited factors.

OTHER SERVICES

(8) Owner acknowledges that Agent has fully explained to Owner the services and marketing activities which Agent has agreed to provide.

REQUIREMENTS FOR PUBLICATION IN MLS COMPILATION

(9) This listing agreement is not acceptable for publication by MLS unless and until the Owner has duly signed this agreement and an acknowledgement reflecting receipt of the definitions of "Exclusive Right to Sell" and "Exclusive Agency" required by the *[Insert applicable law, e.g: New York State Department of State—Division of licensing Services]*.

RENTAL OF PROPERTY

(10) Should the Owner desire to rent the property during the period of this agreement, Agent is hereby granted the sole and exclusive agency to rent the property, exclusive "For Rent" sign privilege and the Owner agrees to pay Agent a rental commission of *[Percentage (x%). The applicable commission for the lease term is due and will be paid upon:*

    (i) The execution of the lease _____

    (ii) The date of occupancy _____

The commission for each and any subsequent renewal thereof, is due and will be paid upon the commencement of each renewal term.

TERMINATION

(11) Owner understands that if Owner terminates the Agent's authority prior to the expiration of its term, Agent shall retain its contract rights (including but not limited to recovery of its commission, advertising expenses and/or any other damages) incurred by reason of an early termination of this agreement.

ADDITIONAL POINTS

(12) Additional Points, of Agreement, if any: *[Specify]*

IN-HOUSE SALES

(13) If the Broker has an agency relationship with the buyer ("buyer's broker"), and that buyer expresses interest in property owned by a seller who also has an agency relationship with the Broker ("seller's broker"), a conflict has arisen. The Broker shall immediately advise both the buyer client and the seller client of the pertinent facts including the fact that a dual agency situation has arisen, and that the following options are available:

(a) The Broker and buyer could dissolve their Agency relationship. The buyer may then seek to retain another broker, and/or an attorney, or may represent himself. This would release the buyer from any Broker employment contract which was entered into with the Broker. Broker may continue to act as agent for the seller.

(b) The Broker and the seller could dissolve their Agency relationship. The seller may then seek to retain another broker, and/or an attorney, or may represent himself. This would release the seller from any listing agreement which was entered into with Broker. The Broker may continue to act as Agent for the buyer.

(c) With fully informed consent, the buyer and seller may elect to continue with the brokerage firm serving as a consensual dual agent, which is the exception to the general rule that agents serve one principal. As a dual agent, the firm and its licensee agents have a duty of fairness to both principals. By mutual agreement the buyer and seller may identify who will negotiate for each principal.

As a dual agent, the firm and its agents cannot furnish undivided loyalty to either party.

As a dual agent, the firm and its licensee agents have a duty not to disclose confidential information given by one principal to the other principal, such as the price one is willing to pay or accept. Such information may already be known to the firm and its agents. If the information is of such a nature that the agent cannot fairly give advice without disclosing it, the agent cannot properly continue to act as an agent.

The buyer, seller and broker shall memorialize the option of their mutual choice by executing a statutory disclosure notice. If there is no mutual agreement, the proposed transaction between buyer and seller shall not be pursued.

ALL MODIFICATIONS TO BE MADE IN WRITING

(14) Owner and Agent agree that no change, amendment, modification or termination of this Agreement shall be binding on any party unless the same shall be in writing and signed by the parties.

DATED: BY: _____
                                [SIGNATURE LINE—OWNER]

DATED: BY: _____
                                [SIGNATURE LINE—AGENT]

FORM 9-4

EXCLUSIVE RIGHT TO SELL AGREEMENT

THIS AGREEMENT is effective as of the _____ day of _____, 20___, and confirms that *[Name of Homeowner]* ("Homeowner") has appointed *[Name of Real Estate Salesperson]* to act as Agent for the sale of property known as *[Address of property being listed for sale]*.

In return for the Agent's agreement to use Agent's best efforts to sell the above property, the Owner agrees to grant the Agent an exclusive right to sell this property under the following terms and conditions:

PERIOD OF AGREEMENT

(1) This agreement shall be effective from the above date and shall expire at midnight on *[Insert Expiration Date]*.

PRICE AT WHICH PROPERTY WILL BE OFFERED AND AUTHORITY

(2) The property will be offered for sale at a list price of *[DOLLAR AMOUNT ($xxx)]* Dollars, and shall be sold, subject to negotiation, at such price and upon such terms to which Owner may agree. The word Owner refers to each and all parties who have ownership interest in the property and the undersigned represents they are the sole and exclusive owners and are fully authorized to enter into this agreement.

COMMISSION TO BE PAID AGENT

(3) The Agent shall be entitled to and Owner shall pay to Agent one commission of *[Percentage (x%)]* of the selling price. Both the Owner and Agent acknowledge that the above commission rate was not suggested nor influenced by anyone other than the parties to this Agreement. Owner hereby authorizes Agent to make an offer of cooperation to any other licensed real estate broker with whom Agent wishes to cooperate. Any commission due for a sale brought about by a Sub-Agent (another broker who is authorized by Agent to assist in the sale of Owner's property) or to an authorized Buyer's Agent shall be paid by the Agent from the commission received by the Agent pursuant to this Paragraph.

The commission offered by Agent to Sub-Agents shall be *[Percentage (Leo)]* of the gross selling price. The commission offered by Agent to Buyer's Agent shall be *[Percentage (Leo)]* of the gross selling price.

In the event that Owner authorizes Agent to compensate a Buyer's Agent, Owner acknowledges Owner's understanding that such Buyer's Agent is not representing Owner as Sub-Agent and that the Buyer's Agent will be representing only the interests of the prospective purchaser.

Owner will not be obligated to pay a commission to Agent if Owner sells Owner's property without the efforts of either Agent, any Sub-Agent or a Buyer's Agent whose services have been authorized by Agent.

OWNER'S OBLIGATIONS AFTER THE EXPIRATION OF THIS AGREEMENT

(4) Owner understands and agrees to pay the commission referred to in paragraph 3, if this property is sold or transferred or is the subject of a contract of sale within _ months after the expiration date of this agreement involving a person with whom the Agent or a Cooperating Broker negotiated or to whom the property was offered, quoted or shown by Agent or any Cooperating Broker during the period of this listing agreement. Owner will not, however, be obligated to pay such commission if Owner enters into a valid Exclusive Listing Agreement with another licensed real estate broker after the expiration of this agreement.

WHO MAY NEGOTIATE FOR OWNER

(5) Owner elects to have all offers submitted through:

   (i) Agent _____

   (ii) Cooperating Agent _____

SUBMISSION OF LISTING TO MULTIPLE LISTING SERVICE

(6) Both Owner and Agent agree that the Agent immediately is to submit this listing agreement to the designated Multiple Listing Service, Inc. ("MLS") for dissemination to its Participants. No provision of this agreement is intended to nor shall be understood to establish or imply any contractual relationship between the Owner and the MLS, nor has the MLS in any way participated in any of the terms of this agreement, including the commission to be paid. Owner acknowledges that the Agent's ability to submit this listing to the MLS, or to maintain such listing amongst those included in any compilation of listing information published by the MLS, is subject to Agent's continued status as a

member in good standing of the designated Board of Realtors, Inc., and Agent's status as a Participant in good standing of the MLS.

FAIR HOUSING

(7) Agent and Owner agree to comply fully with local, state and federal fair housing laws against discrimination on the basis of race, color, religion, sex, national origin, handicap, age, marital status and/or familial status, children or other prohibited factors.

AUTHORIZATION FOR "FOR SALE" SIGN AND OTHER SERVICES

(8) Agent is _ is not _ authorized to place a "For Sale" sign on the property. Owner acknowledges that the Agent has fully explained to Owner the services and marketing activities which Agent has agreed to provide.

REQUIREMENTS FOR PUBLICATION IN MLS COMPILATION

(9) This listing agreement is not acceptable for publication by MLS unless and until the Owner has duly signed this agreement and an acknowledgement reflecting receipt of the definitions of "Exclusive Right to Sell" and "Exclusive Agency" required by the *[Insert applicable law, e.g.: New York State Department of State—Division of licensing Services]*.

RENTAL OF PROPERTY

(10) Should the Owner desire to rent the property during the period of this agreement, Agent is hereby granted the sole and exclusive right to rent the property, exclusive "For Rent" sign privilege and the Owner agrees to pay Agent a rental commission of *[Percentage (x%)]*. The applicable commission for the lease term is due and will be paid upon:

    (i) The execution of the lease _____

    (ii) The date of occupancy _____

The commission for each and any subsequent renewal thereof, is due and will be paid upon the commencement of each renewal term.

TERMINATION

(11) Owner understands that if Owner terminates the Agent's authority prior to the expiration of its term, Agent shall retain its contract rights (including but not limited to recovery of its commission, advertising ex-

penses and/or any other damages) incurred by reason of an early termination of this agreement.

ADDITIONAL POINTS

(12) Additional Points, of Agreement, if any:

IN-HOUSE SALES

(13) If the Broker has an agency relationship with the buyer ("buyer's broker"), and that buyer expresses interest in property owned by a seller who also has an agency relationship with the Broker ("seller's broker"), a conflict has arisen. The Broker shall immediately advise both the buyer client and the seller client of the pertinent facts including the fact that a dual agency situation has arisen, and that the following options are available:

(a) The Broker and buyer could dissolve their Agency relationship. The buyer may then seek to retain another broker, and/or an attorney, or may represent himself. This would release the buyer from any Broker employment contract which was entered into with the Broker. Broker may continue to act as agent for the seller.

(b) The Broker and the seller could dissolve their Agency relationship. The seller may then seek to retain another broker, and/or an attorney, or may represent himself. This would release the seller from any listing agreement which was entered into with Broker. The Broker may continue to act as Agent for the buyer.

(c) With fully informed consent, the buyer and seller may elect to continue with the brokerage firm serving as a consensual dual agent, which is the exception to the general rule that agents serve one principal. As a dual agent, the firm and its licensee agents have a duty of fairness to both principals. By mutual agreement the buyer and seller may identify who will negotiate for each principal.

As a dual agent, the firm and its agents cannot furnish undivided loyalty to either party.

As a dual agent, the firm and its licensee agents have a duty not to disclose confidential information given by one principal to the other principal, such as the price one is willing to pay or accept. Such information may already be known to the firm and its agents. If the information is of such a nature that the agent cannot fairly give advice without disclosing it, the agent cannot properly continue to act as an agent.

The buyer, seller and broker shall memorialize the option of their mutual choice by executing a statutory disclosure notice. If there is no mutual agreement, the proposed transaction between buyer and seller shall not be pursued.

ALL MODIFICATIONS TO BE MADE IN WRITING

(14) Owner and Agent agree that no change, amendment, modification or termination of this Agreement shall be binding on any party unless the same shall be in writing and signed by the parties.

DATED: BY: _____

                             [SIGNATURE LINE—OWNER]

DATED: BY: _____

                             [SIGNATURE LINE—AGENT]

FORM 9-5

REAL ESTATE PURCHASE OPTION CONTRACT

THIS AGREEMENT is made this ___ day of _____, 20___ by and between *[Name]* ("Seller") and *[Name]* ("Buyer"), as follows:

1. Buyer agrees to pay Seller the sum of *[Dollar Amount ($xxx) Dollars]*, as consideration, for the option to purchase the real property owned by Seller located at *[Address of property]* ("property").

2. This option is effective as of the date first written above and will remain in effect until *[Insert Expiration Date]* ("option period"), at which time the option will expire if not previously exercised by Buyer.

3. Buyer hereby has the option and right to purchase said property during the option period stated herein for the sum of *[Dollar Amount ($xxx) Dollars]*.

4. If Buyer exercises the option, the sum of *[Dollar Amount ($xxx) Dollars]* paid as consideration shall be applied to the purchase price stated in paragraph 2.

5. If Buyer elects to exercise his option to purchase said property within the option period, Buyer shall send written notification to Seller by certified or registered mail.

6. This option shall be binding upon and inure to the benefit of the parties, their successors and assigns.

BY: _____
        [SIGNATURE LINE—BUYER]

BY: _____
        [SIGNATURE LINE—SELLER]

FORM 9-6

COMMERCIAL REAL ESTATE LEASE AGREEMENT

This Lease is made on July 1, 2001, by and between ABC Properties (Landlord), with offices located at 500 Main Street, City, State 00000, and John Smith d/b/a Smith's Grocery Store (Tenant), of 123 Main Street, City, State 00000. For valuable consideration, the parties agree as follows:

ARTICLE ONE: DESCRIPTION OF PROPERTY

1. The Landlord agrees to rent to the Tenant the following commercial property:

   a) Property Address:

   b) Description of Property:

   c) Square Feet:

ARTICLE TWO: LEASE TERM

2. The term of this lease will commence on July 1, 2001, until July 1, 2002. Tenant will take immediate possession of the property.

ARTICLE THREE: RENT

3. The monthly rent for the property is [Insert $ Amount] per square foot for a total monthly rent of [Insert $ Amount], the first payment of which is due upon execution of this lease agreement.

4. Rent is payable on the first of each month.

5. There is a grace period of 15 days after which time a late fee in the amount of [Insert $ Amount] will be assessed.

6. If Tenant fails to pay rent on time, Landlord has the right to terminate this lease agreement.

ARTICLE FOUR: CONDITION OF PROPERTY

7. Tenant has inspected the premises and has found the property to be in satisfactory condition. Tenant agrees to maintain the property in

such condition, and to return the property to Landlord, upon expiration of this Lease, in the same condition as when it was first leased by Tenant, and to be responsible for any damages sustained to the property by Tenant during the term of the lease, except for normal wear and tear.

8. Landlord agrees to be responsible for the repair and upkeep of the property exterior and Tenant agrees to be responsible for the repair and upkeep of the property interior.

ARTICLE FIVE: DEPOSITS

9. Upon execution of this lease, Tenant will deposit with Landlord the sum of [Insert $ Amount], which represents a security deposit which will be returned to Tenant within 15 days after termination of the Lease, minus any amounts deducted to cover the repair of any damages sustained to the premises by Tenant, according to Article Four above.

10. Upon execution of this lease, Tenant will deposit with Landlord the sum of [Insert $ Amount], which represents one additional month's rent which will be returned to Tenant within 15 days after termination of the Lease, minus any amounts deducted for rent still outstanding upon termination.

ARTICLE SIX: SERVICES/UTILITIES

11. The Landlord agrees to supply the following services and utilities to Tenant during the term of this lease: (specify)

ARTICLE SEVEN: SUBLEASING

12. Tenant shall not sublet the property without Landlord's written consent, which shall not be unreasonably withheld.

ARTICLE EIGHT: MISCELLANEOUS PROVISIONS

13. This agreement contains the entire understanding of the partners.

14. Any modification of this agreement must be in writing and signed by all of the partners.

15. This Sublease binds and benefits both parties and any successors.

16. Additional Provisions (specify):

Signature Line for Landlord ABC Properties

Signature Line for Tenant John Smith d/b/a Smith's Grocery Store

FORM 9-7

RESIDENTIAL LEASE—SHORT FORM

THIS AGREEMENT, is made this ___ day of _____, 20___ between *[Name of Landlord]* ("Landlord") and *[Name of Tenant]* ("Tenant").

For good and valuable consideration, it is agreed between the above-named parties as follows:

1. Landlord hereby leases and lets to Tenant the premises described as follows: *[Insert address of property being leased]*.

2. This Lease shall be for a term of *[Insert term, e.g., # years, # months, etc.]*, commencing on *[Commencement Date]* and terminating on *[Termination Date]*.

3. Tenant shall pay Landlord the rent of *[Specify dollar amount and manner in which payments are to be made, e.g. Seven Hundred Dollars per month, payable on the first day of each month in advance]*.

4. Tenant shall pay a security deposit of *[Dollar Amount ($xxx)]* dollars, which amount shall be held in an interest-bearing account in *[Name and Address of Bank]*, to be returned upon termination of this lease and full performance of all obligations hereunder, including the payment of all rent due.

5. Tenant shall at his/her own expense provide the following utilities: *[Specify which utilities Tenant shall be liable for, e.g. electricity, gas, water, etc.]*.

6. Landlord shall at its own expense provide the following utilities: *[Specify which utilities Landlord shall be liable for, e.g. electricity, gas, water, etc.]*.

7. Tenant further agrees that upon the termination of the Lease Tenant will return possession of the leased premises in its present condition, reasonable wear and tear excepted. Further, Tenant shall commit no waste to the leased premises.

8. Tenant shall not assign or sublet said premises or allow any other person to occupy the leased premises without Landlord's prior written consent, which consent shall not be unreasonably withheld.

9. Tenant shall not make any material or structural alterations to the leased premises without Landlord's prior written consent.

10. Tenant shall comply with all building, zoning and health codes and other applicable laws for the use of said leased premises.

11. Tenant shall not conduct on premises hazardous activities, or activities deemed a nuisance.

12. Tenant shall not allow pets on the premises *[alternative language: except those specifically set forth herein]*.

13. In the event of any breach of the payment of rent or other breach of this Lease, Landlord shall have full rights to terminate this Lease in accordance with the applicable state law, and enter and reclaim possession of the leased premises, in addition to any other remedies available to Landlord arising from said breach.

14. This Lease shall be binding upon and inure to the benefit of the parties, their successors, assigns and personal representatives.

15. This Lease shall be subordinate to all present or future mortgages against the property.

16. *[Set forth any additional terms agreed to between the parties]*.

BY: _____
       [SIGNATURE LINE—LANDLORD]

BY:_____
       [SIGNATURE LINE—TENANT]

WITNESS:

In the presence of:

_____
   [SIGNATURE LINE—WITNESS]

FORM 9-8

SUBLEASE

This Lease is made on July 1, 2001, by and between John Smith (Tenant), of 123 Main Street, City, State 00000, and Mary Jones (Sub-tenant), of 456 Central Avenue, City, State 00000.

For valuable consideration, the parties agree as follows:

ARTICLE ONE: DESCRIPTION OF PROPERTY

1. The Tenant agrees to sublease to the Sub-tenant the following property:

   a) Property Address:

   b) Description of Property:

ARTICLE TWO: CURRENT TERMS AND CONDITIONS

2. The above-described property is currently leased to Tenant under the terms of the following described lease, a copy of which is attached hereto: (describe terms and conditions of current lease)

ARTICLE THREE: SUBLEASE TERM

3. The term of this sublease will commence on July 1, 2001, until July 1, 2002. Sub-tenant will take immediate possession of the property.

ARTICLE FOUR: RENT

4. The monthly subrental payment for the property is [Insert $ Amount] per month, the first payment of which is due upon execution of this lease agreement.

5. Rent is payable on the first of each month.

ARTICLE FIVE: MISCELLANEOUS PROVISIONS

6. Tenant represents that the underlying lease agreement is in effect and permission to sublet this property is authorized. A copy of such permission from Landlord is attached hereto.

7. Tenant agrees to indemnify and hold Sub-tenant harmless from any claim which may result from Tenant's failure to perform under Tenant this lease prior to execution of this Sublease.

8. Sub-tenant agrees to indemnify and hold Tenant harmless from any claim which may result from Sub-tenant's failure to perform under the this lease subsequent to execution of this Sublease.

9. Sub-tenant agrees to perform all obligations and duties of Tenant under the original lease, and sub-tenant shall receive all benefits of Tenant under the original lease.

10. Tenant agrees to remain liable to Landlord for all obligations under the terms and conditions of the original lease.

11. This agreement contains the entire understanding of the partners.

12. Any modification of this agreement must be in writing and signed by all of the partners.

13. This Sublease binds and benefits both parties and any successors.

14. Additional Provisions (specify):

Signature Line for Tenant John Smith

Signature Line for Sub-tenant Mary Jones

FORM 9-9

COMPLAINT BY TENANT FOR BREACH OF WARRANTY OF HABITABILITY

NAME OF COURT

NAME OF JURISDICTION

COMPLAINT

Plaintiff, John Jones, by his attorney, _____, as and for his Complaint against the defendant, alleges as follows:

1. At all times hereinafter mentioned, plaintiff was a resident of the County of _____, State of _____.

2. At all times hereinafter mentioned, defendant was a resident of the County of _____, State of _____.

3. At all times hereinafter mentioned, defendant was the owner of a residential apartment building located at _____ _____.

4. At all times hereinafter mentioned, plaintiff was a tenant of the defendant, and occupied an apartment known as _____, located on the fifth floor of said apartment building.

5. At all times hereinafter mentioned, the defendant breached its warranty of habitability of the leased premises in that the ceiling tiles located in the living room of said apartment were loose, and that this condition had been in existence prior to the occurrence herein complained of, and that defendant had actual and constructive knowledge of this problem.

6. On _____, 19___, plaintiff was sitting in his living room when one of the ceiling tiles fell on his head, causing him to suffer severe injuries to his head and neck, all or some of which may be permanent.

7. Said injuries were caused by the failure of defendant to properly maintain the premises, and defendant's breach of warranty of habitability of the leased premises.

8. The plaintiff in no way contributed to his injuries.

WHEREFORE, plaintiff seeks judgment against the defendant in the sum of _____ ($xxx) Dollars, together with the costs and disbursements of this action, and for such other and further relief as the Court deems proper.

BY: _____

[SIGNATURE LINE—ATTORNEY FOR PLAINTIFF]

FORM 9-10

NOTICE TO LANDLORD OF TENANT'S INTENTION TO VACATE LEASED PREMISES

[Date]

[Via Certified Mail—Return Receipt Requested]

Landlord's Name

Street Address

City, State Zip Code

Re: Notice of Intention to Vacate Leased Premises Located at [Address]

As set forth in our lease dated _____, I hereby notify you of my intention to vacate said premises on _____, 2001. Please forward the security deposit to me in care of the following address:

_____.

By:_____

    [Signature Line—Tenant]

FORM 9-11

THREE-DAY NOTICE TO TENANT TO VACATE THE LEASED PREMISES DUE TO NON-PAYMENT OF RENT

[Date]

[Via Certified Mail—Return Receipt Requested]

Tenant's Name

Street Address

City, State Zip Code

Re: Three-Day Notice to Vacate Leased Premises Located at [Address]

You are hereby notified to surrender the above-referenced leased premises you occupy as our tenant and to vacate said premises on or within three days of your receipt of this notice, as a consequence of your non-payment of rent due under the lease.

The present rent due and owing in connection with said lease is _____ [$xxx] Dollars. This notice may be rescinded upon full payment of said amount within three days of your receipt of this notice.

If you fail to pay all rent payments due and owing, we will have no recourse but to seek immediate legal action to evict you from said premises and to seek damages and attorneys' fees and costs as prescribed by law.

By:_____
    [Signature Line—Landlord]

FORM 9-12

BUYER'S ESTIMATED CLOSING COSTS

ITEM	ESTIMATED AMOUNT	ACTUAL AMOUNT
(1) Application Fee: Charged by Lender	May range from $100 - $300	$_____
(2) Appraisal Fee	Approximately $250	$_____
(3) Credit Report	Approximately $50	$_____
(4) Escrow Fees (Insurance): Amounts paid to lender for insurance	Generally includes advance payments of homeowner's insurance (2 months); and flood and PMI insurance when required (2 months)	$_____
(5) Escrow Fees (Taxes): Amounts paid to lender for property and school taxes	Generally includes advance (3 months)	$_____
(6) Flood Certification Fee: Required by lender to verify flood zone status of property	Approximately $15.	$_____
(7) Flood Insurance,Varies depending on flood zone	Generally $500 - $1000 per year	$_____
(8) Funding Fee	a percentage of the loan amount charged on VA loans instead of PMI	$_____
(9) Home Inspection	Approximately $300 - $500	$_____
(10) Homeowner's Insurance	Varies, generally .0025 of purchase price per year	$_____

(11) Buyer's Legal Fees	Legal fees vary depending on attorney and location, but generally range from $750 - $1,000	$_____
(12) Lender's Legal Fee: For review of documents	Ranges from $150 - $250, where applicable	$_____
(13) Mortgage Tax	Generally 0.75% of mortgage amount, where applicable	$_____
(14) Points: Amount paid to lender to "buydown" interest rate on mortgage	Usually ranges from 0 to 3 points	$_____
(15) Prepaid Interest	Interest on mortgage payable to lender from date of closing to end of 1st month	$_____
(16) Private Mortgage Insurance: PMI is required if mortgage is more than 80% of purchase price	Generally .004 of mortgage amount	$_____
(17) Recording Fees	Approximately $50 - $75	$_____
(18) Survey	Depends on size of property, but ranges from $350 - $500	$_____
(19) Title Insurance	Approximately $500 per $100,000 of coverage	$_____
(20) Title Search	Approximately $150 - $200	$_____
ESTIMATED TOTAL CLOSING COSTS:		$_____

FORM 9-13

BUYER'S MORTGAGE PAYMENT ESTIMATION CHART

INTEREST RATE (%)	10 YEARS	15 YEARS	20 YEARS	25 YEARS	30 YEARS
5.00	$10.61	$7.91	$ 6.60	$5.85	$ 5.37
5.25	$10.73	$8.04	$6.74	$5.99	$5.52
5.50	$10.85	$8.17	$6.88	$6.14	$5.68
5.75	$10.98	$8.30	$7.02	$6.29	$5.84
6.00	$11.10	$8.44	$7.16	$6.44	$6.00
6.25	$11.23	$8.57	$7.31	$6.60	$6.16
6.50	$11.35	$8.71	$7.46	$6.75	$6.32
6.75	$11.48	$8.85	$7.60	$6.91	$6.49
7.00	$11.61	$8.99	$7.75	$7.07	$6.65
7.25	$11.74	$9.13	$7.90	$7.23	$6.82
7.50	$11.87	$9.27	$8.06	$7.39	$6.99
7.75	$12.00	$9.41	$8.21	$7.55	$7.16
8.00	$12.13	$9.56	$8.36	$7.72	$7.34
8.25	$12.27	$9.70	$8.52	$7.88	$7.51
8.50	$12.40	$9.85	$8.68	$8.05	$7.69
8.75	$12.53	$9.99	$8.84	$8.22	$7.87
9.00	$12.67	$10.14	$9.00	$8.39	$8.05
9.25	$12.80	$10.29	$9.16	$8.56	$8.23
9.50	$12.94	$10.44	$9.32	$8.74	$8.41
9.75	$13.08	$10.59	$9.49	$8.91	$8.59
10.00	$13.22	$10.75	$9.65	$9.09	$8.78

DIRECTIONS FOR ESTIMATING MONTHLY MORTGAGE PAYMENTS:

Select the interest rate and term for the mortgage loan you are considering to ascertain your monthly payment per $1000 of loan principal. For example, if you are considering a mortgage loan in the amount of $50,000 which carries an interest rate of 7.50% for a term of 30 years, multiply the indicated amount of $6.99 by 50 ($50,000/100). Thus, $349.50 is the estimated monthly payment not including taxes, insurance or miscellaneous closing costs.

CHAPTER 10
COPYRIGHT, PATENT AND TRADEMARK

FORM 10-1

LETTER REQUESTING PERMISSION TO USE COPYRIGHTED MATERIALS

TO: [Publisher Name and Address]

Dear [Insert Name]:

I am writing to ask your permission to incorporate into a printed publication the following material:

[Describe material, e.g., name of book/article; name of author; page number(s), etc.].

The material will be distributed/published as follows:

[Describe intended use of material, e.g., name of publication; publisher; publication date, etc.].

If you do not solely control the copyright in the requested material, please provide with co-publisher information so that I can obtain the necessary joint approvals.

Thank you.

FORM 10-2

NON-EXCLUSIVE COPYRIGHT LICENSE

COPYRIGHT LICENSE

This Agreement (the "Agreement") is made by and between [Name of Copyright Owner] ("Owner"), and [Name of Licensee] ("Licensee") with its principal place of business at [Insert Address].

RECITALS

1. Licensee is [describe entity], engaged in [describe business activity relevant to copyrighted material].

2. Owner owns the copyright to certain copyrighted materials and is willing to allow Licensee to copy and utilize such materials under the terms herein set forth.

NOW THEREFORE, in consideration of the mutual covenants and promises herein contained, the Owner and Licensee agree as follows:

1. This Agreement shall be effective as of (the "Effective Date").

2. Owner hereby grants Licensee a non-exclusive right to copy certain copyrighted materials described in Exhibit A (the "Copyrighted Material"), in whole or in part, and to incorporate the Copyrighted Material, in whole or in part, into other works (the "Derivative Works") for Licensee's use only.

3. All right, title and interest in the Copyrighted Material, including without limitation, any copyright, shall remain with Owner.

4. Owner shall also own the copyright in the Derivative Works.

5. This Agreement may be terminated by the written agreement of both parties. In the event that either party shall be in default of its material obligations under this Agreement and shall fail to remedy such default within sixty (60) days after receipt of written notice thereof, this Agreement shall terminate upon expiration of the sixty (60) day period.

6. Exhibit A is incorporated herein and made a part hereof for all purposes.

7. This Agreement constitutes the entire and only agreement between the parties and all other prior negotiations, agreements, representations and understandings are superseded hereby.

8. This Agreement shall be construed and enforced in accordance with the laws of the United States of America and of the State of New York.

IN WITNESS WHEREOF, the parties have executed this Agreement, effective this _____ day of _____, 20___ .

_____
OWNER/LICENSOR

_____
LICENSEE

FORM 10-3

ASSIGNMENT OF COPYRIGHT

This Agreement is made between XYZ CORPORATION ("Assignee") and JOHN SMITH ("Author), whose address is [Insert Address]. Author represents and warrants that he/she is the sole creator and owner of [describe work] (the "Work"), designed and created for the Assignee's Public Relation's Department, and holds the complete and undivided copyright interest to the Work.

For valuable consideration, receipt and sufficiency of which are hereby acknowledged, Author and Assignee agree as follows:

Author does hereby sell, assign, and transfer to Assignee, its successors and assigns, the entire right, title and interest in and to the copyright in the Work and any registrations and copyright applications relating thereto and any renewals and extensions thereof, and in and to all works based upon, derived from, or incorporating the Work, and in an to all income, royalties, damages, claims and payments now or hereafter due or payable with respect thereto, and in and to all causes of action, either in law or in equity for past, present, or future infringement based on the copyrights, and in and to all rights corresponding to the foregoing throughout the world.

2. Author agrees to execute all papers and to perform such other proper acts as Assignee may deem necessary to secure for Assignee or its designee the rights herein assigned.

IN WITNESS WHEREOF, the parties have executed this Agreement, effective this _____ day of _____, 20___ .

XYZ CORPORATION, ASSIGNEE:

_____

Name/Title

AUTHOR:

_____

Name/SSN

FORM 10-4

WORK MADE FOR HIRE AGREEMENT

This Agreement made the_____day of _____, 20____, by and between JOHN SMITH ("Employee") and XYZ CORPORATION ("Employer").

THE AUTHOR AND THE EMPLOYER AGREE THAT:

1. Title and Copyright Assignment

(a) Author and Employer intend this to be a contract for services and each considers the products and results of the services to be rendered by Author hereunder to be a work made for hire (the "Work").

(b) Author acknowledges and agrees that the Work, and all rights therein including, without limitation, copyright, belongs to and shall be the sole and exclusive property of Employer.

(c) If for any reason the Work would not be considered a work made for hire under applicable law, Author does hereby sell, assign, and transfer to Employer, its successors and assigns, the entire right, title and interest in and to the copyright in the Work and any registrations and copyright applications relating thereto and any renewals and extensions thereof, and in and to all works based upon, derived from, or incorporating the Work, and in an to all income, royalties, damages, claims and payments now or hereafter due or payable with respect thereto, and in and to all causes of action, either in law or in equity for past, present, or future infringement based on the copyrights, and in and to all rights corresponding to the foregoing throughout the world.

(d) If the Work is one to which the provisions of 17 U.S.C. 106A apply, the Author hereby waives and appoints Employer to assert on the Author's behalf the Author's moral rights or any equivalent rights regarding the form or extent of any alteration to the Work including, without limitation, removal or destruction, or the making of any derivative works based on the Work, including, without limitation, photographs, drawings or other visual reproductions or the Work, in any medium, for Employer purposes.

(e) Author agrees to execute all papers and to perform such other proper acts as Employer may deem necessary to secure for Employer or its designee the rights herein assigned.

2. Delivery

(a) The Author will deliver to the Employer on or before [Insert Date] the completed Work in form and content satisfactory to the Employer.

(b) If the Author fails to deliver the Work on time, the Employer will have the right to terminate this agreement and to recover from the Author any sums advanced in connection with the Work. Upon such termination, the Author may not have the Work published elsewhere until such advances have been repaid.

3. Permission to Use Copyrighted Material

With the exception works in the public domain or works which constitute fair use, the Work will contain no material from other copyrighted works without a written consent of the copyright holder. Any obligations associated with obtaining such permissions will be the responsibility of the Author.

4. Warranty and Indemnification

The Author warrants that he or she is the sole owner of the Work and has full power and authority to make this agreement; that the Work does not infringe any copyright, violate any property rights, or contain any scandalous, libelous, or unlawful matter. The Author will defend, indemnify, and hold harmless the Employer and/or its licensees against all claims, suits, costs, damages, and expenses that the Employer and/or its licensees may sustain by reason of any scandalous, libelous, or unlawful matter contained or alleged to be contained in the Work or any infringement or violation by the Work of any copyright or property right; and until such claim or suit has been settled or withdrawn, the Employer may withhold any sums due the Author under this agreement.

5. Consideration

In consideration for delivery of the Work in accordance with the provisions of this Agreement, Employer shall pay Author [Insert Dollar Amount] within 30 days of receipt and acceptance of the Work.

6. Term

This agreement shall remain in effect for one (1) year from its effective date.

7. Default

In the event that either party shall be in default of its material obligations under this agreement and shall fail to remedy such default within sixty (60) days after receipt of written notice thereof, this agreement shall terminate upon expiration of the sixty (60) day period.

8. Miscellaneous

(a) The written provisions contained in this agreement constitute the sole and entire agreement made between the Author and the Employer concerning this Work, and any amendments to this agreement shall not be valid unless made in writing and signed by both parties.

(b) This agreement shall be construed and interpreted according to the laws of the State of New York and shall be binding upon the parties hereto, their heirs, successors, assigns, and personal representatives; and references to the Author and to the Employer shall include their heirs, successors, assigns, and personal representatives.

IN WITNESS WHEREOF, the parties have executed this Agreement, effective this _____ day of _____, 20___ .

XYZ CORPORATION, EMPLOYER:

_____
Name/Title

EMPLOYEE:

_____
Name/SSN

FORM 10-5

COPYRIGHT APPLICATION—FORM PA (PERFORMING ARTS)

FEE CHANGES
Fees are effective through June 30, 2002. After that date, check the Copyright Office Website at www.loc.gov/copyright or call (202) 707-3000 for current fee information.

FORM PA
For a Work of the Performing Arts
UNITED STATES COPYRIGHT OFFICE

REGISTRATION NUMBER

PA   PAU

EFFECTIVE DATE OF REGISTRATION

Month   Day   Year

DO NOT WRITE ABOVE THIS LINE. IF YOU NEED MORE SPACE, USE A SEPARATE CONTINUATION SHEET.

1 TITLE OF THIS WORK ▼

PREVIOUS OR ALTERNATIVE TITLES ▼

NATURE OF THIS WORK ▼ See instructions

2 **a** NAME OF AUTHOR ▼

DATES OF BIRTH AND DEATH
Year Born ▼   Year Died ▼

Was this contribution to the work a "work made for hire"?
☐ Yes
☐ No

AUTHOR'S NATIONALITY OR DOMICILE
Name of Country
OR { Citizen of ▶
Domiciled in ▶

WAS THIS AUTHOR'S CONTRIBUTION TO THE WORK
Anonymous? ☐ Yes ☐ No
Pseudonymous? ☐ Yes ☐ No
If the answer to either of these questions is "Yes," see detailed instructions.

NATURE OF AUTHORSHIP Briefly describe nature of material created by this author in which copyright is claimed. ▼

NOTE

Under the law, the "author" of a "work made for hire" is generally the employer, not the employee (see instructions). For any part of this work that was "made for hire" check "Yes" in the space provided, give the employer (or other person for whom the work was prepared) as "Author" of that part, and leave the space for dates of birth and death blank.

b NAME OF AUTHOR ▼

DATES OF BIRTH AND DEATH
Year Born ▼   Year Died ▼

Was this contribution to the work a "work made for hire"?
☐ Yes
☐ No

AUTHOR'S NATIONALITY OR DOMICILE
Name of Country
OR { Citizen of ▶
Domiciled in ▶

WAS THIS AUTHOR'S CONTRIBUTION TO THE WORK
Anonymous? ☐ Yes ☐ No
Pseudonymous? ☐ Yes ☐ No
If the answer to either of these questions is "Yes," see detailed instructions.

NATURE OF AUTHORSHIP Briefly describe nature of material created by this author in which copyright is claimed. ▼

c NAME OF AUTHOR ▼

DATES OF BIRTH AND DEATH
Year Born ▼   Year Died ▼

Was this contribution to the work a "work made for hire"?
☐ Yes
☐ No

AUTHOR'S NATIONALITY OR DOMICILE
Name of Country
OR { Citizen of ▶
Domiciled in ▶

WAS THIS AUTHOR'S CONTRIBUTION TO THE WORK
Anonymous? ☐ Yes ☐ No
Pseudonymous? ☐ Yes ☐ No
If the answer to either of these questions is "Yes," see detailed instructions.

NATURE OF AUTHORSHIP Briefly describe nature of material created by this author in which copyright is claimed. ▼

3 **a** YEAR IN WHICH CREATION OF THIS WORK WAS COMPLETED
This information must be given
◀ Year in all cases.

b DATE AND NATION OF FIRST PUBLICATION OF THIS PARTICULAR WORK
Complete this information
ONLY if this work
has been published.
Month ▶ _____ Day ▶ _____ Year ▶ _____
◀ Nation

4 COPYRIGHT CLAIMANT(S) Name and address must be given even if the claimant is the same as the author given in space 2. ▼

See instructions before completing this space.

TRANSFER If the claimant(s) named here in space 4 is (are) different from the author(s) named in space 2, give a brief statement of how the claimant(s) obtained ownership of the copyright. ▼

APPLICATION RECEIVED

ONE DEPOSIT RECEIVED

TWO DEPOSITS RECEIVED

FUNDS RECEIVED

DO NOT WRITE HERE
OFFICE USE ONLY

MORE ON BACK ▶ • Complete all applicable spaces (numbers 5-9) on the reverse side of this page.
• See detailed instructions.   • Sign the form at line 8.

DO NOT WRITE HERE
Page 1 of _____ pages

EXAMINED BY	FORM PA
CHECKED BY	
☐ CORRESPONDENCE Yes	FOR COPYRIGHT OFFICE USE ONLY

DO NOT WRITE ABOVE THIS LINE. IF YOU NEED MORE SPACE, USE A SEPARATE CONTINUATION SHEET.

PREVIOUS REGISTRATION Has registration for this work, or for an earlier version of this work, already been made in the Copyright Office?

☐ Yes ☐ No If your answer is "Yes," why is another registration being sought? (Check appropriate box.) ▼ If your answer is "no," go to space 7.

a. ☐ This is the first published edition of a work previously registered in unpublished form.

b. ☐ This is the first application submitted by this author as copyright claimant.

c. ☐ This is a changed version of the work, as shown by space 6 on this application.

If your answer is "Yes," give: **Previous Registration Number ▼**   **Year of Registration ▼**

5

DERIVATIVE WORK OR COMPILATION Complete both space 6a and 6b for a derivative work; complete only 6b for a compilation.

Preexisting Material Identify any preexisting work or works that this work is based on or incorporates. ▼

a

6

See instructions before completing this space.

Material Added to This Work Give a brief, general statement of the material that has been added to this work and in which copyright is claimed. ▼

b

DEPOSIT ACCOUNT If the registration fee is to be charged to a Deposit Account established in the Copyright Office, give name and number of Account.

Name ▼   **Account Number ▼**

a

7

CORRESPONDENCE Give name and address to which correspondence about this application should be sent.   Name/Address/Apt/City/State/ZIP ▼

b

Area code and daytime telephone number ▶ (   )   Fax number ▶ (   )

Email ▶

CERTIFICATION* I, the undersigned, hereby certify that I am the

Check only one ▶

☐ author

☐ other copyright claimant

☐ owner of exclusive right(s)

☐ authorized agent of _____

Name of author or other copyright claimant, or owner of exclusive right(s) ▲

of the work identified in this application and that the statements made by me in this application are correct to the best of my knowledge.

8

Typed or printed name and date ▼ If this application gives a date of publication in space 3, do not sign and submit it before that date.

Date ▶

Handwritten signature (X) ▼

☞   X _____

Certificate will be mailed in window envelope to this address:	Name ▼
	Number/Street/Apt ▼
	City/State/ZIP ▼

YOU MUST:
• Complete all necessary spaces
• Sign your application in space 8

SEND ALL 3 ELEMENTS IN THE SAME PACKAGE:
1. Application form
2. Nonrefundable filing fee in check or money order payable to *Register of Copyrights*
3. Deposit material

MAIL TO:
Library of Congress
Copyright Office
101 Independence Avenue, S.E.
Washington, D.C. 20559-6000

As of July 1, 1999, the filing fee for Form PA is $30.

9

*17 U.S.C. § 506(e): Any person who knowingly makes a false representation of a material fact in the application for copyright registration provided for by section 409, or in any written statement filed in connection with the application, shall be fined not more than $2,500.   ♲ PRINTED ON RECYCLED PAPER   ☉U.S. GOVERNMENT PRINTING OFFICE: 1999-454-879/56

June 1999—200,000
WEB REV: June 1999

FORM 10-6

COPYRIGHT APPLICATION—FORM SR (SOUND RECORDINGS)

Fees are effective through June 30, 2002. After that date, check the Copyright Office Website at www.loc.gov/copyright or call (202) 707-3000 for current fee information.

FORM SR
For a Sound Recording
UNITED STATES COPYRIGHT OFFICE

REGISTRATION NUMBER

SR   SRU
EFFECTIVE DATE OF REGISTRATION

Month   Day   Year

DO NOT WRITE ABOVE THIS LINE. IF YOU NEED MORE SPACE, USE A SEPARATE CONTINUATION SHEET.

1 TITLE OF THIS WORK ▼

PREVIOUS, ALTERNATIVE, OR CONTENTS TITLES (CIRCLE ONE) ▼

2 a NAME OF AUTHOR ▼

DATES OF BIRTH AND DEATH
Year Born ▼   Year Died ▼

Was this contribution to the work a "work made for hire"?
□ Yes
□ No

AUTHOR'S NATIONALITY OR DOMICILE
Name of Country
OR { Citizen of ▶
Domiciled in ▶

WAS THIS AUTHOR'S CONTRIBUTION TO THE WORK
Anonymous? □ Yes □ No
Pseudonymous? □ Yes □ No
If the answer to either of these questions is "Yes," see detailed instructions.

NATURE OF AUTHORSHIP Briefly describe nature of material created by this author in which copyright is claimed. ▼

NOTE

Under the law, the "author" of a "work made for hire" is generally the employer, not the employee (see instructions). For any part of this work that was "made for hire," check "Yes" in the space provided, give the employer (or other person for whom the work was prepared) as "Author" of that part, and leave the space for dates of birth and death blank.

b NAME OF AUTHOR ▼

DATES OF BIRTH AND DEATH
Year Born ▼   Year Died ▼

Was this contribution to the work a "work made for hire"?
□ Yes
□ No

AUTHOR'S NATIONALITY OR DOMICILE
Name of Country
OR { Citizen of ▶
Domiciled in ▶

WAS THIS AUTHOR'S CONTRIBUTION TO THE WORK
Anonymous? □ Yes □ No
Pseudonymous? □ Yes □ No
If the answer to either of these questions is "Yes," see detailed instructions.

NATURE OF AUTHORSHIP Briefly describe nature of material created by this author in which copyright is claimed. ▼

c NAME OF AUTHOR ▼

DATES OF BIRTH AND DEATH
Year Born ▼   Year Died ▼

Was this contribution to the work a "work made for hire"?
□ Yes
□ No

AUTHOR'S NATIONALITY OR DOMICILE
Name of Country
OR { Citizen of ▶
Domiciled in ▶

WAS THIS AUTHOR'S CONTRIBUTION TO THE WORK
Anonymous? □ Yes □ No
Pseudonymous? □ Yes □ No
If the answer to either of these questions is "Yes," see detailed instructions.

NATURE OF AUTHORSHIP Briefly describe nature of material created by this author in which copyright is claimed. ▼

3 a YEAR IN WHICH CREATION OF THIS WORK WAS COMPLETED
This information must be given
◀ Year in all cases.

b DATE AND NATION OF FIRST PUBLICATION OF THIS PARTICULAR WORK
Complete this information ONLY if this work has been published.
Month ▶ _____ Day ▶ _____ Year ▶ _____
◀ Nation

4 a COPYRIGHT CLAIMANT(S) Name and address must be given even if the claimant is the same as the author given in space 2. ▼

See instructions before completing this space.

APPLICATION RECEIVED

ONE DEPOSIT RECEIVED

TWO DEPOSITS RECEIVED

FUNDS RECEIVED

DO NOT WRITE HERE OFFICE USE ONLY

b TRANSFER If the claimant(s) named here in space 4 is (are) different from the author(s) named in space 2, give a brief statement of how the claimant(s) obtained ownership of the copyright. ▼

MORE ON BACK ▶   • Complete all applicable spaces (numbers 5-9) on the reverse side of this page.
    • See detailed instructions.   • Sign the form at line 8.

DO NOT WRITE HERE
Page 1 of _____ pages

EXAMINED BY	FORM SR
CHECKED BY	
CORRESPONDENCE ❑ Yes	FOR COPYRIGHT OFFICE USE ONLY

DO NOT WRITE ABOVE THIS LINE. IF YOU NEED MORE SPACE, USE A SEPARATE CONTINUATION SHEET.

PREVIOUS REGISTRATION Has registration for this work, or for an earlier version of this work, already been made in the Copyright Office?

❑ Yes ❑ No If your answer is "Yes," why is another registration being sought? (Check appropriate box) ▼

a. ❑ This work was previously registered in unpublished form and now has been published for the first time.

b. ❑ This is the first application submitted by this author as copyright claimant.

c. ❑ This is a changed version of the work, as shown by space 6 on this application.

If your answer is "Yes," give: **Previous Registration Number** ▼   **Year of Registration** ▼

5

DERIVATIVE WORK OR COMPILATION

a Preexisting Material Identify any preexisting work or works that this work is based on or incorporates. ▼

b Material Added to This Work Give a brief, general statement of the material that has been added to this work and in which copyright is claimed. ▼

6

See instructions
before completing
this space.

DEPOSIT ACCOUNT If the registration fee is to be charged to a Deposit Account established in the Copyright Office, give name and number of Account.

a Name ▼   Account Number ▼

b **CORRESPONDENCE** Give name and address to which correspondence about this application should be sent.   Name/Address/Apt/City/State/ZIP ▼

Area code and daytime telephone number ▶   Fax number ▶

Email ▶

7

CERTIFICATION* I, the undersigned, hereby certify that I am the

Check only one ▼

❑ author

❑ other copyright claimant

❑ owner of exclusive right(s)

❑ authorized agent of _____
    Name of author or other copyright claimant, or owner of exclusive right(s) ▲

of the work identified in this application and that the statements made by me in this application are correct to the best of my knowledge.

Typed or printed name and date ▼ If this application gives a date of publication in space 3, do not sign and submit it before that date.

_____ Date ▶ _____

Handwritten signature (x) ▼

X _____

8

Certificate will be mailed in window envelope to this address	Name ▼
	Number/Street/Apt ▼
	City/State/ZIP ▼

YOU MUST:
• Complet: all necessary spaces
• Sign your application in space 8
SEND ALL 3 ELEMENTS
IN THE SAME PACKAGE:
1. Application form
2. Nonrefundable filing fee in check or money order payable to *Register of Copyrights*
3. Deposit material
MAIL TO:
Library of Congress
Copyright Office
101 Independence Avenue, S.E.
Washington, D.C. 20559-6000

As of
July 1, 1999,
the filing fee
for Form SR
is $30.

9

FORM 10-7

COPYRIGHT RENEWAL APPLICATION—FORM RE

Fees are effective through June 30, 2002. After that date, check the Copyright Office Website at www.loc.gov/copyright or call (202) 707-3000 for current fee information.

FORM RE
For Renewal of a Work
UNITED STATES COPYRIGHT OFFICE

REGISTRATION NUMBER

EFFECTIVE DATE OF RENEWAL REGISTRATION

Month	Day	Year

DO NOT WRITE ABOVE THIS LINE. IF YOU NEED MORE SPACE, USE A SEPARATE CONTINUATION SHEET.

1

RENEWAL CLAIMANT(S), ADDRESS(ES), AND STATEMENT OF CLAIM ▼   (See Instructions)

a
Name ....
Address ....
Claiming as ....
(Use appropriate statement from instructions)

b
Name ....
Address ....
Claiming as ....

c
Name ....
Address ....
Claiming as ....

2

TITLE OF WORK IN WHICH RENEWAL IS CLAIMED ▼

RENEWABLE MATTER ▼

PUBLICATION AS A CONTRIBUTION If this work was published as a contribution to a periodical, serial, or other composite work, give information about the collective work in which the contribution appeared.   Title of Collective Work ▼

If published in a periodical or serial give: Volume ▼   Number ▼   Issue Date ▼

3

AUTHOR(S) OF RENEWABLE MATTER ▼

4

ORIGINAL REGISTRATION NUMBER ▼   ORIGINAL COPYRIGHT CLAIMANT ▼

ORIGINAL DATE OF COPYRIGHT

If the original registration for this work was made in published form, give: If the original registration for this work was made in unpublished form, give:

DATE OF PUBLICATION: _____   **OR**   DATE OF REGISTRATION: _____
(Month)   (Day)   (Year)   (Month)   (Day)   (Year)

MORE ON BACK ▶   • Complete all applicable spaces (numbers 5-8) on the reverse side of this page.   DO NOT WRITE HERE
• See detailed instructions.   • Sign the form at space 7.   Page 1 of _____ pages

RENEWAL APPLICATION RECEIVED	FORM RE
CORRESPONDENCE ❑ YES	
EXAMINED BY	FOR
CHECKED BY	COPYRIGHT OFFICE USE
FUNDS RECEIVED	ONLY

DO NOT WRITE ABOVE THIS LINE. IF YOU NEED MORE SPACE, USE A SEPARATE CONTINUATION SHEET (FORM RE/CON).

RENEWAL FOR GROUP OF WORKS BY SAME AUTHOR: To make a single registration for a group of works by the same individual author published as contributions to periodicals (see instructions), give full information about each contribution. If more space is needed, request continuation sheet (Form RE/CON).

5

a
Title of Contribution: ....
Title of Periodical: .... Vol: .... No: .... Issue Date: ....
Date of Publication: .... Registration Number: ....
(Month) (Day) (Year)

b
Title of Contribution: ....
Title of Periodical: .... Vol: .... No: .... Issue Date: ....
Date of Publication: .... Registration Number: ....
(Month) (Day) (Year)

c
Title of Contribution: ....
Title of Periodical: .... Vol: .... No: .... Issue Date: ....
Date of Publication: .... Registration Number: ....
(Month) (Day) (Year)

d
Title of Contribution: ....
Title of Periodical: .... Vol: .... No: .... Issue Date: ....
Date of Publication: .... Registration Number: ....
(Month) (Day) (Year)

6

DEPOSIT ACCOUNT: If the registration fee is to be charged to a Deposit Account established in the Copyright Office, give name and number of Account.

Name _____

Account Number _____

Area code and daytime telephone number ▶ _____

CORRESPONDENCE: Give name and address to which correspondence about this application should be sent.

Name _____

Address _____ (Apt)

_____ (City) _____ (State) _____ (ZIP)

Fax number ▶ _____ Email Address ▶ _____

7

CERTIFICATION* I, the undersigned, hereby certify that I am the: (Check one)
❑ renewal claimant ❑ duly authorized agent of _____
(Name of renewal claimant) ▲
of the work identified in this application and that the statements made by me in this application are correct to the best of my knowledge.

Typed or printed name ▼ _____ Date ▼ _____

☞ Handwritten signature (X) ▼ _____

8

Certificate will be mailed in window envelope to this address:

Name ▼ _____
Number/Street/Apt ▼ _____
City/State/ZIP ▼ _____

YOU MUST:
• Complete all necessary spaces
• Sign your application in space 7

SEND ALL ELEMENTS IN THE SAME PACKAGE:
1. Application form
2. Nonrefundable filing fee in check or money order payable to Register of Copyrights

MAIL TO:
Library of Congress
Copyright Office
101 Independence Avenue, S.E.
Washington, D.C. 20559-6000

As of July 1, 1999, the filing fee for Form RE is $45.

December 1999—20,000   ♳ PRINTED ON RECYCLED PAPER   ☆U.S. GOVERNMENT PRINTING OFFICE: 2000-461-113/87
WEB REV: December 1999

FORM 10-8

DECLARATION FOR PATENT APPLICATION

PTO/SB/01 (03-01)
Approved for use through 10/31/2002. OMB 0651-0032
U.S. Patent and Trademark Office; U.S. DEPARTMENT OF COMMERCE
Under the Paperwork Reduction Act of 1995, no persons are required to respond to a collection of information unless it contains a valid OMB control number.

DECLARATION FOR UTILITY OR DESIGN PATENT APPLICATION (37 CFR 1.63)	Attorney Docket Number	
	First Named Inventor	
	COMPLETE IF KNOWN	
	Application Number	/
☐ Declaration Submitted with Initial Filing **OR** ☐ Declaration Submitted after Initial Filing (surcharge (37 CFR 1.16 (e)) required)	Filing Date	
	Group Art Unit	
	Examiner Name	

As a below named inventor, I hereby declare that:

My residence, mailing address, and citizenship are as stated below next to my name.

I believe I am the original, first and sole inventor (if only one name is listed below) or an original, first and joint inventor (if plural names are listed below) of the subject matter which is claimed and for which a patent is sought on the invention entitled:

(Title of the Invention)

the specification of which

☐ is attached hereto

OR

☐ was filed on (MM/DD/YYYY) [_____] as United States Application Number or PCT International

Application Number [_____] and was amended on (MM/DD/YYYY) [_____] (if applicable).

I hereby state that I have reviewed and understand the contents of the above identified specification, including the claims, as amended by any amendment specifically referred to above.

I acknowledge the duty to disclose information which is material to patentability as defined in 37 CFR 1.56, including for continuation-in-part applications, material information which became available between the filing date of the prior application and the national or PCT international filing date of the continuation-in-part application.

I hereby claim foreign priority benefits under 35 U.S.C. 119(a)-(d) or (f), or 365(a) of any foreign application(s) for patent, inventor's or plant breeder's rights certificate(s), or 365(a) of any PCT international application which designated at least one country other than the United States of America, listed below and have also identified below, by checking the box, any foreign application for patent, inventor's or plant breeder's rights certificate(s), or any PCT international application having a filing date before that of the application on which priority is claimed.

Prior Foreign Application Number(s)	Country	Foreign Filing Date (MM/DD/YYYY)	Priority Not Claimed	Certified Copy Attached? YES	NO
			☐	☐	☐
			☐	☐	☐
			☐	☐	☐
			☐	☐	☐

☐ Additional foreign application numbers are listed on a supplemental priority data sheet PTO/SB/02B attached hereto:

[Page 1 of 2]

Burden Hour Statement: This form is estimated to take 21 minutes to complete. Time will vary depending upon the needs of the individual case. Any comments on the amount of time you are required to complete this form should be sent to the Chief Information Officer, U.S. Patent and Trademark Office, Washington, DC 20231. DO NOT SEND FEES OR COMPLETED FORMS TO THIS ADDRESS. SEND TO: Assistant Commissioner for Patents, Washington, DC 20231.

PTO/SB/01 (03-01)
Approved for use through 10/31/2002. OMB 0651-0032
U.S. Patent and Trademark Office; U.S. DEPARTMENT OF COMMERCE
Under the Paperwork Reduction Act of 1995, no persons are required to respond to a collection of information unless it contains a valid OMB control number.

DECLARATION — Utility or Design Patent Application

Direct all correspondence to: ☐	Customer Number or Bar Code Label		OR ☐	Correspondence address below

Name

Address

City	State	ZIP

Country	Telephone	Fax

I hereby declare that all statements made herein of my own knowledge are true and that all statements made on information and belief are believed to be true; and further that these statements were made with the knowledge that willful false statements and the like so made are punishable by fine or imprisonment, or both, under 18 U.S.C. 1001 and that such willful false statements may jeopardize the validity of the application or any patent issued thereon.

NAME OF SOLE OR FIRST INVENTOR : ☐ A petition has been filed for this unsigned inventor

Given Name (first and middle [if any])	Family Name or Surname	

Inventor's Signature		Date

Residence: City	State	Country	Citizenship

Mailing Address

City	State	ZIP	Country

NAME OF SECOND INVENTOR: ☐ A petition has been filed for this unsigned inventor

Given Name (first and middle [if any])	Family Name or Surname	

Inventor's Signature		Date

Residence: City	State	Country	Citizenship

Mailing Address

City	State	ZIP	Country

☐ Additional inventors are being named on the ____supplemental Additional Inventor(s) sheet(s) PTO/SB/02A attached hereto.

[Page 2 of 2]

FORM 10-9

ASSIGNMENT OF PATENT APPLICATION

Sample Form (former PTO/SB/15) (05-01)

ASSIGNMENT OF APPLICATION	Docket Number (Optional)

Whereas, I/We, _____ of _____ ,hereafter

referred to as applicant, have invented certain new and useful improvements in _____

_____

☐ for which an application for a United States Patent was filed on _____

Application Number _____ /_____ .

☐ for which an application for a United States Patent was executed on _____ , and

Whereas, _____ of _____ herein referred

to "assignee" whose mailing address is _____ is

desirous of acquiring the entire right, title and interest in the same;

Now, therefore, in consideration of the sum of _____ dollars ($ _____), the receipt whereof is acknowledged, and other good and valuable consideration, I/We, the applicant(s), by these presents do sell, assign and transfer unto said assignee the full and exclusive right to the said invention in the United States and the entire right, title and interest in and to any and all Patents which may be granted therefor in the United States, I/We hereby authorize and request the Commissioner of Patent and Trademarks to issue said United States Patent to said assignee, of the entire right, title, and interest in and to the same, for his sole use and behoof; and for the use and behoof of his legal representatives, to the full end of the term for which said Patent may be granted, as fully and entirely as the same would have been held by me had this assignment and sale not been made.

Executed this _____ day of _____ , 20 _____ .

at _____ .

State of _____)

County of _____)   SS:

Before me personally appeared said _____

and acknowledged the foregoing instrument to be his free act and deed this _____

day of _____ , 20 _____ .

_____
(Signature)

Seal   (Notary Public)

Note: Signatures of all the inventors or assignees of record of the entire interest or their representative(s) are required. Submit multiple forms if more than one signature is required, See below*.

* ☐ Total of _____ forms are submitted.

This form offers a sample or suggested format for an assignment document. This sample form is not an OMB officially approved form.

FORM 10-10

COMPLAINT REGARDING INVENTION PROMOTER

PTO/SB/2048
Approved for use through 07/31/00. OMB 0651-0044
Patent and Trademark Office; U.S. DEPARTMENT OF COMMERCE
Under the Paperwork Reduction Act of 1995, no persons are required to respond to a collection of information unless it
displays a valid OMB control number.

COMPLAINT REGARDING INVENTION PROMOTER

Instructions: Read the reverse side of this form before completing and submitting the form. Complete as
much of the form as possible and return it to the U.S. Patent and Trademark Office at the address given on
the reverse side. Please type or write clearly.

Invention Promoter's Name: _____Telephone # _____

Invention Promoter's Address: _____

City_____State_____Zip Code _____

Complainant's Name: _____ Telephone # _____

Complainant's Address: _____ _____

City_____State_____Zip Code _____

Customer's Name: _____

WHAT IS YOUR COMPLAINT?

Please be as specific as possible. Specify the invention promotion services offered to be performed or
performed, provide the name of the mass media in which the invention promoter advertised as providing
such services, and explain the relationship between the customer and the invention promoter. If additional
space is needed, the information may be provided on paper attached to this form.

_____

_____

_____

_____

_____

_____

_____

_____

_____

Signed: _____ Date: _____

Burden Hour Statement: This collection of information is provided for by 35 U.S.C. § 297(d). The information regarding invention
promoters will be released to the public. This form is estimated to take 15 minutes to complete. This time will vary depending upon
the needs of the individual case. Any comments on the amount of time you are required to complete this form should be sent to the
Chief Information Officer, Patent and Trademark Office, Washington, D.C. 20231. DO NOT SEND FEES OR COMPLETED
FORMS TO THIS ADDRESS.

PRIVACY ACT STATEMENT

Section 297 of Title 35, United States Code, authorizes collection of this information. The primary use of this information is to make complaints publicly available. Additional disclosures will be made to (i) persons or entities identified in the complaint, and (ii) a Federal, State, or local law enforcement agency.

Furnishing the information on this form is voluntary, but failure to submit the information may prevent the communication from being a publicly available complaint.

Carefully read the following:

An 'Invention Promoter" is defined in 35 U.S.C. § 297(c)(3) as "any person, firm, partnership, corporation, or other entity who offers to perform or performs invention promotion services for, or on behalf of, a customer, and who holds out itself through advertising in any mass media as providing such services, but does not include

    (A) any department or agency of the Federal Government or of a State or local government;

    (B) any nonprofit, charitable, scientific, or educational organization, qualified under applicable State law or described under section 170(b)(1)(A) of the Internal Revenue Code;

    (C) any person or entity involved in the evaluation to determine commercial potential of, or offering to license or sell, a utility patent or a previously filed nonprovisional utility patent application;

    (D) any party participating in a transaction involving the sale of the stock or assets of a business; or

    (E) any party who directly engages in the business of retail sales of products or the distribution of products."

'Invention Promotion Services" is defined in 35 U.S.C. § 297(c)(4) as 'the procurement or attempted procurement for a customer of a firm, corporation, or other entity to develop and market products or services that include the invention of the customer."

'Customer" is defined in 35 U.S.C. § 297(c)(2) as "any individual who enters into a contract with an invention promoter for invention promotion services."

'Contract for invention promotion services" is defined in 35 U.S.C. § 297(c)(1) as "a contract by which an invention promoter undertakes invention promotion services for a customer."

Any individual completing and filing the complaint form should understand the following.

    1. No action will be taken by the U.S. Patent and Trademark Office on behalf of the individual against the invention promoter based on the complaint. The U.S. Patent and Trademark Office has no authority to pursue a cause of action on behalf of any individual against an invention promoter or provide the individual with any personal remedy. If an individual believes that he or she has an actionable case, the individual should consult with an attorney about the possible legal options which may be available.

    2. The complaint will be published.

    3. The U.S. Patent and Trademark Office will provide the invention promoter with a reasonable opportunity to respond.

    4. The response by the invention promoter will be published.

Submit your complaint form by mail to:

    U. S. Patent and Trademark Office
    Office of Independent Inventor Programs
    Box 24
    Washington, D.C. 20231

FORM 10-11

APPLICATION TO REGISTER A TRADEMARK

NYS DEPARTMENT OF STATE
MISCELLANEOUS RECORDS
41 State Street
Albany, NY 12231-0001

REG NO

Original Application to Register a Trademark

Please read the instructions prior to completing this form; attach additional sheets as needed.

1. APPLICANT NAME

2. ADDRESS   NUMBER AND STREET   CITY   STATE   ZIP

3. IF A CORPORATION, ENTER STATE IN WHICH INCORPORATED AND
   IF A PARTNERSHIP, ENTER STATE IN WHICH ORGANIZED

4. IF A PARTNERSHIP, LIST THE NAMES OF ALL GENERAL PARTNERS

5. DESCRIBE THE TRADEMARK, INCLUDING A WRITTEN DESCRIPTION OF DESIGN FEATURES, IF ANY (DO NOT GLUE A FACSIMILE TO THIS FORM)

6. DESCRIBE THE SPECIFIC GOODS BEING PRODUCED ON WHICH THE TRADEMARK IS USED

7. STATE THE MANNER IN WHICH THE TRADEMARK IS PLACED ON THE GOODS, CONTAINERS, ETC.

8. CLASS NUMBER(S)   9. DATE OF   (A) IN NEW YORK STATE   (B) ELSEWHERE
                                              FIRST USE

FOR OFFICE USE ONLY

The applicant is the owner of the mark, the mark is in use, and, to the knowledge of the person
verifying the application, no other person has registered, either federally or in this state, or has the right
to use such mark either in the identical form or in such near resemblance as to be likely, when applied
to the goods of such other person, to cause confusion, or to cause mistake, or to deceive.

The undersigned applies to register the aforesaid mark pursuant to Article 24 of the General Business
Law and affirms under the penalties of perjury that the statements herein made, including any
attached papers, are true.

(Corporation, Association, Firm, etc.)

By: _____
    (Signature and Title of Officer)   *(Date)*

DOS-241 (REV. 2/98)

FORM 10-12

NOTICE OF OPPOSITION TO TRADEMARK REGISTRATION

Suggested Format for Notice of Opposition

(This is a suggested format for preparing a Notice of Opposition. This document is not meant to be used as a form to be filled in and returned to the Board. Rather, it is a suggested format, which shows how the Notice of Opposition should be set up. Opposers may follow this format in preparing their own Notice of Opposition but need not copy those portions of the suggested format which are not relevant.)

IN THE UNITED STATES PATENT AND TRADEMARK OFFICE
BEFORE THE TRADEMARK TRIAL AND APPEAL BOARD

In the matter of trademark application Serial No............................
For the mark...
Published in the Official Gazette on........(Date)...........................

(Name of opposer)
        v.
(Name of applicant)

NOTICE OF OPPOSITION

State opposer's name, address, and entity information as follows.[1]

(Name of individual as opposer, and business trade name, if any;
Business address)

OR   (Name of partnership as opposer; Names of partners;
                Business address of partnership)

OR   (Name of corporation as opposer; State or country of incorporation;
                Business address of corporation)

The above-identified opposer believes that it/he/she will be damaged by registration of the mark shown in the above-identified application, and hereby opposes the same.[2]

The grounds for opposition are as follows:

[Please set forth, in separately numbered paragraphs, the allegations of opposer's standing and grounds for opposition.][3]

By _____ (Signature)[4] _____   Date_____
     (Identification of person signing)[5]

OMB No. 0651-0009 (Exp. 8/31/01)

FORM 10-13

PETITION TO CANCEL A TRADEMARK REGISTRATION

Suggested Format for Petition to Cancel

This is a suggested format for preparing a Petition to Cancel a trademark registration. This document is not meant to be used as a form to be filled in and returned to the Board. Rather, it is a suggested format, which shows how the petition should be set up. Petitioners may follow this format in preparing their own petition but need not copy those portions of the suggested format which are not relevant.

IN THE UNITED STATES PATENT AND TRADEMARK OFFICE
BEFORE THE TRADEMARK TRIAL AND APPEAL BOARD

In the matter of trademark Registration No...............................
For the mark..
Date registered.............................

(Name of petitioner)
v.
(Name of registrant)

PETITION TO CANCEL

State petitioner's name, address, and entity information as follows:[1]

(Name of individual as petitioner, and business trade name, if any;
Business address)

OR   (Name of partnership as petitioner; Names of partners;
Business address of partnership)

OR   (Name of corporation as petitioner; State or country of incorporation;
Business address of corporation)

To the best of petitioner's knowledge, the name and address of the current owner of the registration are _____ *(provide if known)* _____

The above-identified petitioner believes that it/he/she will be damaged by the above-identified registration, and hereby petitions to cancel the same.[2]

The grounds for cancellation are as follows:
[Please set forth, in separately numbered paragraphs, the allegations of petitioner's standing and grounds for cancellation][3]

By ____ Signature[4] ____   Date _____
(Identification of person signing)[5]

OMB No. 0651-0041 (Exp. 1/31/01)

CHAPTER 11
MISCELLANEOUS LEGAL FORMS

FORM 11-1

ACKNOWLEDGEMENT—CORPORATION

STATE OF)

        ss.:

COUNTY OF)

On the _____ day of _____, 20___, before me personally came *[Name]*, who being by me duly sworn, did depose and say that he is the *[Insert Corporate Title, e.g., President]* of *[Insert Name of Corporation]*, the corporation described in and which executed the foregoing instrument; that he/she knows the seal of said corporation; that the seal affixed is such corporate seal; that it was so affixed by order of the Board of Directors of said corporation, and that he/she signed his/her name thereto by like order.

_____

    [NOTARY PUBLIC]

FORM 11-2

ACKNOWLEDGEMENT—INDIVIDUAL

STATE OF   )

                 : ss.:

COUNTY OF   )

On the _____ day of _____, 20___, before me personally came *[Name]*, to me known to be the individual described in and who executed the foregoing instrument, and acknowledged that he/she executed the same.

_____

     [NOTARY PUBLIC]

FORM 11-3

GENERAL POWER OF ATTORNEY

I, *[Name of Grantor]*, residing at *[Address]*, hereby appoint *[Name]* of *[Address]*, as my Attorney-in-Fact ("Attorney-in-Fact").

I hereby revoke any and all general powers of attorney that previously have been signed by me.

My Attorney-in-Fact shall have full power and authority to act on my behalf. This power and authority shall authorize my Attorney-in-Fact to manage and conduct all of my affairs and to exercise all of my legal rights and powers, including all rights and powers that I may acquire in the future. My Attorney-in-Fact's powers shall include, but not be limited to, the power to:

1. Open, maintain or close bank accounts (including, but not limited to checking accounts, savings accounts, and certificates of deposit), brokerage accounts, and other similar accounts with financial institutions.

2. Sell, exchange, buy, invest, or reinvest any assets or property owned by me.

3. Purchase and/or maintain insurance, including life insurance upon my life.

4. Take any and all legal steps necessary to collect any amount or debt owed to me, or to settle any claim, whether made against me or asserted on my behalf against any other person or entity.

5. Enter into binding contracts on my behalf.

6. Exercise all stock rights on my behalf as my proxy.

7. Maintain and/or operate any business that I may own, and

8. Employ professional and business assistance as may be appropriate, including attorneys, accountants, and real estate agents.

9. Sell, convey, lease, mortgage, manage, insure, improve, repair, or perform any other act with respect to any of my property.

10. Prepare, sign, and file documents with any governmental body or agency, including but not limited to the preparation, signing and filing

---

of income and other tax returns with federal, state and local governmental bodies.

This is a General Power of Attorney and the listing of specific powers is not intended to limit or restrict the general powers granted.

My Attorney-in-Fact shall not be liable for any loss that results from a judgment error that was made in good faith. However, my Attorney-in-Fact shall be liable for willful misconduct or the failure to act in good faith while acting under the authority of this Power of Attorney.

My Attorney-in-Fact shall not be entitled to any compensation, during my lifetime or upon my death, for any services provided as my Attorney-in-Fact. My Attorney-in-Fact shall be entitled to reimbursement of all reasonable expenses incurred in connection with this Power of Attorney.

My Attorney-in-Fact shall provide an accounting for all funds handled and all acts performed as my Attorney-in-Fact, if I so request, or if such a request is made by any authorized personal representative or fiduciary acting on my behalf.

This Power of Attorney shall become effective immediately and shall continue effective until my death and may be revoked by me at any time by providing written notice to my Attorney-in-Fact.

DATED: BY: _____

                                 [SIGNATURE LINE-GRANTOR]

STATE OF   )

                       ss.:

COUNTY OF   )

On the _____ day of _____, 20___, before me personally came *[Name]*, to me known to be the individual described in and who executed the foregoing instrument, and acknowledged that he/she executed the same.

_____
[NOTARY PUBLIC]

FORM 11-4

LIMITED POWER OF ATTORNEY

TO ALL PERSONS, be it known, that I, *[Name of Grantor]*, of *[Address]*, as Grantor, do hereby grant a limited and specific power of attorney to *[Name of Attorney-In-Fact]*, of *[Address]*, as my *attorney-in-fact.*

My named attorney-in-fact shall have full power and authority to undertake and perform the following acts on my behalf to the same extent as if I had done so personally:

[Specify powers the attorney-in-fact is being granted]

The authority granted shall include such incidental acts as are reasonably required or necessary to carry out and perform the specific authorities and duties stated herein.

My attorney-in-fact agrees to accept this appointment subject to its terms, and agrees to act and perform in said fiduciary capacity consistent with my best interests as s/he in her/his discretion deems advisable, and I ratify all acts so carried out.

This power of attorney may be revoked by me at any time, and shall automatically be revoked upon my death, provided any person relying on this power of attorney before or after my death shall have full rights to accept the authority of my attorney-in-fact consistent with the powers granted until in receipt of actual notice of revocation.

I have hereunto signed my name this _____ day of _____, 20___.

BY: _____
[SIGNATURE OF GRANTOR]

STATE OF   )

            ss.:

COUNTY OF   )

On the _____ day of _____, 20___, before me personally came *[Name of Grantor]*, to me known and known to me to be the individual described in, and who executed the foregoing, and duly acknowledged to me that s/he executed the same.

_____
[NOTARY PUBLIC]

FORM 11-5

REVOCATION OF POWER OF ATTORNEY

I, *[Name]*, of *[Address]*, hereby revoke any and all powers of attorney previously signed by me, without regard to the identity of the party or parties designated in such documents to act on my behalf.

DATED: BY:_____

                               [SIGNATURE LINE]

STATE OF   )

                ss.:

COUNTY OF   )

On the _____ day of _____, 20___ before me personally came *[Name]*, to me known to be the individual described in and who executed the foregoing instrument, and acknowledged that he/she executed the same.

_____
       [NOTARY PUBLIC]